HeartBreak Therapy

HeartBreak Therapy

Repair Manual for a Broken Heart

Andrew Gentile

Mill City Press, Minneapolis

Mill City Press, Inc.
322 First Avenue N, 5th floor
Minneapolis, MN 55401
612.455.2293
www.millcitypublishing.com

ISBN-13: 978-1-62652-388-3
LCCN: 2013916314

Cover graphic by Alberto J. Palacios
Illustrations by Robert Gentile
Book Design by Mary Kristin Ross

Printed in the United States of America

MILL CITY PRESS

Disclaimer

This book was designed to help individuals wishing to help themselves and is not meant to replace the work of a professional therapist or counselor. For individuals with a diagnosis of a mental illness, implementation of the techniques provided in this book and the accompanying audio should only be done under the guidance of a mental health professional.

Every effort has been made to make this book as complete as possible given the nature of the topic. Much of this book contains information based on the experience of the author, who does not claim that each article of information has been empirically studied or proven. Doing so would preclude sharing this valuable information.

This book is for educational purposes only. The author and publisher shall have neither liability nor responsibility to any person or entity with respect to any loss or damage caused or alleged to be caused directly or indirectly by the information contained in this book.

A deep love resides inside each of us. This love is independent of the desires, thoughts, and opinions, good or bad, which are readily offered to us. It is a love that is gentle and kind, accepting and nonjudgmental, playful and spontaneous, courageous and curious. It is always encouraging and always evolving. This love can be discovered only through turning off the noise around us, coming to ourselves in silence, meditation, and prayer. If we listen carefully, we will hear the murmurs of our inner voice tell yearnings of our truest selves. What is available to us is a profound understanding, appreciation, and full acceptance of self, all of the good and all of the bad.

Only when we truly know that we are able to tap into this part of ourselves can we begin to love others fully. Love for others is the manifestation of love for self. We cannot love another more than we love ourselves. Life is a mirror. If you want to know what love for yourself looks like, look at your love for others. If you want to know what your love for others look like, look at your love for self. When you love yourself this way, you love God this way. This relationship is the divine love triangle: self, God, and others in any order.

—*Marlon Hartley Lindsay*

Acknowledgments

This book could never have happened without all of the broken hearts that have been brought to me over the years by all of my beautiful clients. It was their tears-turned-smiles and their imprisonments-turned-liberations that inspired my own heart to share this work with the world. I honor their honesty, their openness, and their commitment to themselves that they displayed in seeking a better life experience. Each of these clients taught me something about the nature of the heart, the nature of heartache, and the methods that help in its healing. I am especially grateful to Andrew Childers, who upon hearing my idea for this book insisted that I make it a reality.

I am also grateful to those whom I have loved and to those for whom I have allowed my heart to break. It was in the loving that I learned the most about the heart and love, and it was in the breaking that I learned the most about heartache and the pathways to healing. Some of the techniques presented in *HeartBreak Therapy* were refined partly from using them to extricate myself from periods of emotional turmoil resulting from breakups, while others are commonly found within the repertoire of hypnotherapists and Neuro-Linguistic Programming practitioners everywhere.

Thank you to my teachers, Marlene Mulder and Randall Churchill, at the Hypnotherapy Training Institute. Your heart-centered training many years ago gave me the skills to bring healing to so many and provided a foundation of love and integrity that continues to weave its way through my work and my philosophy.

Thank you to those dear friends who believed in this project and volunteered their time to review, edit, and provide feedback on the various iterations of this text: Erika Atkinson, Karin Ott Kristensen, and Stefana Serafina. Thank you to Alberto Palacios, who designed the cover graphic out of the kindness of his soul, and to my genius and comedic brother, Robert, for generously enlivening the book with his playful illustrations, asking nothing in return but to simply join me on this adventure.

Lastly, I give thanks to my loving partner, Andrew Nolan, who is not only a brilliant healer, but who unceasingly teaches me and inspires me to think bigger and bolder.

Introduction

The ending of a loving relationship can be one of the most devastating of human experiences. Romantic heartbreak is often experienced as a shock to the system on par with other human tragedies, such as death, war, disease, and natural disasters. And while these other forms of human tragedies are commonly acknowledged and commemorated with societal gatherings (funerals, cleanup efforts) and interventions (relief efforts, compensation, grief counseling), when we lose a loved one through the ending of a relationship, we are commonly left to our own emotional survival skills to sort ourselves out. For most people, emotional survival skills are at a minimum, and all too often heartache sufferers end up in addiction, depression, or worse.

It is my hope that *HeartBreak Therapy* offers a healthy healing pathway to those with nowhere else to turn and that it provides an expanded array of therapeutic options and perspectives on a topic that gets far too little attention from mainstream mental health practitioners.

It is also my hope that the book and audio format of

HeartBreak Therapy provides a new model for other hypnotherapists and neuro-linguistic programmers to explain their beautiful and powerful healing work to the layperson and to bring the mechanisms behind these healing modalities out of the shrouds of mystery and into the light of day.

—*Andrew Gentile*

Chapter 1

My Experience Working with Heartache

My greatest joy in life is helping to alleviate suffering. Working with heartache has been one of the most satisfying aspects of my hypnotherapy practice. I am always humbled and honored when a client seeks my help in rising out of their pain into a more peaceful state of being.

Clients seeking help with heartache often arrive in great distress, feeling torn up inside, and are often embarrassed at their loss of self-control, both emotionally and behaviorally. Most of us have been there—these experiences are well known to anyone who has had an unrequited crush, a broken first romance, or any intense love connection that came to an end. We are often obsessed with our former partner's activities and sometimes engage in stalker-type behavior, even though such compulsions are completely out of alignment with our typical day-to-day personalities and ethics. These out-of-character feelings and compulsions are often overwhelming, and they give us a feeling that we have lost touch with who we are. This sense of being out of control emotionally deals a major blow to our self-esteem and our self-confidence.

I always assure my clients that what they are experiencing is completely normal and that I, too, have been in their shoes, as has most anyone who has had a full emotional and interpersonal life.

There is a great bliss that clients experience upon swinging from feelings of pain and sadness into the freedom of emotional independence that is achieved when the heartache is released. The contrast between these two emotional states is astounding. To see my clients making that full transition with a single technique is pure magic. Seeing this transformation happen time and again has been one of the highlights of my work.

Many of my clients "snap out" of their heartache within a single session, usually through a single therapeutic process that can take as little as fifteen minutes. Given that heartache has been one of the most easily resolved conditions I have worked with, I knew that a lot of people could benefit from these techniques being made available in a book and audio self-help format.

While many of these techniques will be familiar to those who study and practice hypnotherapy and Neuro-Linguistic Programming (NLP), this is the first time they have been consolidated into a format intended for the end user who is seeking release from heartache.

Each of the techniques in this book has helped my clients to move beyond heartache. While it often only takes one of these techniques to do the trick, each person and each situation is unique, so a single approach cannot be counted on to work every time for every person. For this reason, I have included ten different techniques to increase the potential for a quick recovery. Similarly, the success of these techniques is also dependent upon each individual's baseline self-esteem, self-image, core beliefs and values, and emotional patterns that were often established in childhood, as well as one's ability to follow guided instructions, to relax, and to surrender themselves fully into the guided processes and visualizations.

The set of guided processes featured here draws from the best of hypnotherapy and NLP therapeutic techniques. They are tools of self-discovery and transformation, are reproducible, and do not require an expert or experienced individual to apply them. These tools are safe and easy to use.

Chapter 2

Welcome to the Heart

Sadness flies on the wings of the morning
and out of the heart of darkness comes the light.

—Jean Giraudoux

Western medicine has well established the physiological role of the heart as the focal point of life in the human body. Electrochemical reactions in the nerves and muscles of the heart allow us to have a heartbeat, which pumps blood through our circulatory system, delivering nutrients and carrying away wastes. When it comes to physiological life, the heart is even more important than the brain: the body may be kept alive even after brain death, as long as the heart continues to function.

While science acknowledges the heart as the focal point of human physiological life, humanity as a whole has long established the role of the heart as the center of emotional life. This role is evidenced through the poignant representations of the heart in music, poetry, and the arts. The heart is the primary representative of love, the master of all emotions. During times of great loss, we often experience this emotional center through physical pain in the heart area. A broken heart hurts.

Metaphysics also acknowledges the role of the heart as an energetic or electromagnetic center, testifying that the energetic vortex of the heart chakra is in the middle of the seven master chakras, with three chakras above and another three below it. Conventional scientists also agree that the continuous electrochemical activity in the heart gives it the strongest electromagnetic field of any organ or system in the body.

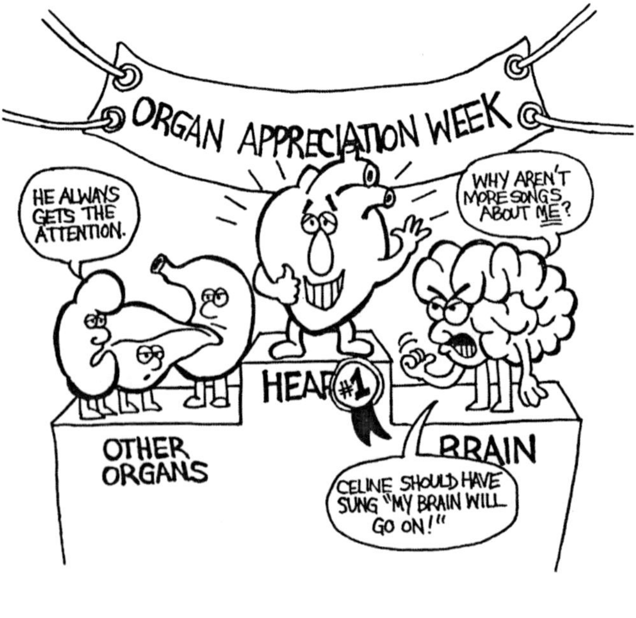

To western medicine, the heart is no more than a mechanical pump, and the purpose of treating any form of heart disease is to maintain proper blood flow to the various organs and systems of the body. But what about disease in the emotional or electromagnetic aspects of the heart? What are the relationships between these various functions? Why is it that when we experience intense grief, we feel pain in our chest and palpitations in the heart? Can healing a broken heart on the emotional level bring healing to our heart on other levels?

From "Heartbreak" to "Heartache"

We know for certain that bringing emotional healing to a broken heart is profoundly beneficial on the psychological and emotional levels. A broken heart can be debilitating, often causing us to hit the "pause" button on life. Healing this condition allows us to hit "play" once again. Emotional states are expressed in the body through physiology and neurochemistry. Alleviating emotional stress, such as a broken heart, brings not only emotional relief, but also physical relief. The body can rest, sleep, relax, smile, laugh, and do all the other good things that are well-established contributors to health and longevity.

When we hear or read words, our brains translate them into images and feelings so that they can be understood holographically and encoded into our memory in tangible terms. Our imagination takes words and translates them into 3-D holograms that we place ourselves in for a moment. For example, when you consider the words "car crash," immediately you are able to visualize both an accident from the outsider's view and also imagine the bodily pain and trauma of being inside a crashing car. This brief example shows the power of the words that we choose.

The language we use in the healing process is very important. The term "broken heart" usually evokes an image of a heart actually split in two. Since this book is intended to bring healing, we are going to use a softer term that implies a milder starting point, one that can be more easily healed. For the rest of this book, we will replace "heartbreak" with "heartache." The heart is simply experiencing discomfort (ache) and needs a little help coming back into healthy functioning.

One of the simplest and most fundamental steps in healing is developing a clear mental picture of your goal: in this case, your healed heart. As simple as this might seem, you may be surprised at how instantly this helps you.

Take a moment now, close your eyes, take a few deep breaths, and focus your attention upon your heart.

Imagine your heart being big and strong, beating with a regular rhythm, feeding your whole body, and sending strong electromagnetic fields into a space that extends eight feet around your body.

Take a few more deep breaths as you focus on this image.

Imagine your heart as the "master organ" in your body. See and feel your heart as a central control transceiver for all the organs and systems in your body. Imagine the electromagnetic fields that it sends out as communicating with all organs and systems in your body, synchronizing them all, bringing them all into harmony.

Take a few more deep breaths as you focus on this image. Then return to your space and open your eyes.

Chapter 3

How this Healing System Works

The purpose of this system is to bring fast and effective release (not just relief) from heart discomfort associated with the ending of a relationship.

The primary healing offered through this system is that of returning you to a state of self-love. Heartache is painful because you are either clinging to a source of external love that had been feeding you emotionally but has been removed or to an object of your love that has been taken from your grasp, giving your outflow of love nowhere to land. Sometimes you have lost both. This system aims to return both the source and object of your love to yourself; by using it, you should have an increased ability to receive love from yourself and to give love to yourself.

Heartache also often hurts because of how we interpret the ending of the relationship and how it changes our views of ourselves or of others and the world. These are usually erroneous conclusions that need correcting back into a healthy, balanced, and realistic view of how and why romantic relationships form and dissolve. The typical erroneous conclusions from breakups are also addressed here.

This book provides ten different techniques for healing heartache. Since each case of heartache is unique, a variety of techniques are offered. It is my hope that everyone is able to gain some healing from this system, no matter the level or flavor of heartache. Some of the techniques will resonate with you and others may not. The system is designed for you to review the techniques in print and then select the ones that are best matched for you to experience in the audio format (explained later).

You may want to use several of the techniques or only one of them. You may want to start with one that seems to be a match for your current emotional state and needs. As your healing progresses, you may find that you are ready for another technique for another layer of healing. Healing through the layers of heartache, as with many personal exploration and healing paths, can be like peeling an onion. As you resolve one layer, you reveal another layer underneath. This is an exciting process that can teach you a lot about yourself and will bring you increasing degrees of emotional awareness, emotional intelligence, and freedom.

Some of the techniques involve tasks for you to complete on your own and include step-by-step instructions, while others are guided processes like mini-hypnotherapy sessions or guided visualizations. For the guided processes, audio versions are available for you to download from the downloads page on http://www.heartbreaktherapy.com/ (enter password "healheartnow"). The audio files are recordings of me leading you through the processes in the book. Alternatively, you can have a local hypnotherapist or someone close to you guide you through these processes by reading them to you from this book. Another option is to record them using your own voice and to then play them back to yourself. If you wish to work with me directly, either in person or by Skype, you can contact me via www.HeartBreakTherapy.com.

Chapter 4

Background on Heartache

Heartache is an emotional state that is the result of feeling abandoned or rejected. It can include feelings of sadness and isolation. It can be difficult to describe the nuance and intensity of emotional pain that can accompany heartache. Several of these feelings can combine to result in depression and anxiety.

When emotionally healthy individuals with a strong sense of self experience heartache, they can usually recover within a reasonable timeframe and return after weeks or months to a balanced emotional state with their original sense of self and world intact. However, when the emotional pain is deep and intense enough, or when the foundational self-esteem or attitudes are already compromised, heartache can extend from months to years and represent a dramatic decrease in quality of life.

In the worst cases, heartache can cause deep and long-lasting shifts in beliefs about the self, the world, relationships, and the ability to trust. In such cases, recovery from heartache essentially does not occur, and those affected are likely to live out the rest of their lives in pain, with a lack of trust and a cynical attitude, feeling wary about connecting romantically for fear of being hurt.

Heartache can have short-term and long-term consequences for our quality of life (our self-worth/self-esteem/self-love), on our other relationships, on our personal productivity, and on our abilities to love and make meaningful contributions to the world. Healing heartache is not only about healing the individual; it is also about bringing collective healing to the communities that we form and to the planet at large. The more we live from a loving, open heart, the greater the ripple effect we each have on the world around us. As we heal our own hearts, we heal the collective heart.

Before we examine the nature of heartache, let's take a deeper look at the nature of the heart. We first need to understand and appreciate the heart as the place in our body where love is felt. It is not simply a romanticized notion that the heart represents love, romance, and compassion. The concept of the heart being our love-center is a truth that civilizations throughout history have acknowledged based on observation of the human experience.

Perhaps the most developed and well-known concept of the heart as a center for love is provided in the sacred religious texts of India: the Vedas and the Upanishads. The ancient Hindu teachings acknowledge that our physical bodies have an underlying energy body. Within this energy body are seven chakras, wheel-like energy vortices, each one associated with its own set of physical, emotional, mental, and spiritual issues and attributes. The heart area is associated with the heart chakra. The heart chakra is associated with complex emotions, compassion, tenderness, unconditional love, equilibrium, rejection, and well-being. According to this ancient perspective, the heart chakra governs physical circulation in the body; emotionally, it fosters empathy and unconditional love for the self and others; mentally, it is in charge of passion; and spiritually, it is the seat of devotion.

Prior to the development of modern science, "educated" humans generally viewed the human system as a single, integrated system. The development of individual sciences, such as biology and psychology, led to the fields of physical medicine and mental health, and from that developed a faulty perception that the body is a system that is distinct and separate from that of the mind. Neither biologists nor psychologists learn about the interplay of emotions and physiology. Emotions were practically left out altogether and relegated to being a byproduct of the mind, and the "mind-body connection" is a topic left for the fluffy metaphysical crowd.

The development of the Western scientific model in "Enlightenment Era" Europe destroyed the long-standing understanding of the mind-body connection that had been the main healing perspective for tens of thousands of years. The era of rationalism brought about a thinking model that considered all indigenous methods of healing to be primitive, superstitious, fraudulent, and sometimes downright satanic. Indigenous healing methods practiced by the pre-Christian peoples of Europe were destroyed through witch hunts, inquisitions, and various other forms of violence, intimidation, and ethnic cleansing.

With the passage of time, Western science has found that the long-standing Newtonian scientific model falls apart. Emotions and other phenomena of consciousness simply cannot be explained or measured without opening to new (or old!) paradigms and methods. Western science is slowly coming full circle to once again embrace many of the more holistic concepts of health and healing that the very same institution swore against during its earliest beginnings.

Increasingly, researchers are turning to alternative healing methods and philosophies, most of which are rooted in ancient wisdoms that have survived the rationalist takeover. The development of quantum physics is changing the scientific paradigm to begin to embrace the concept of non-locality (telepathy, remote healing, the power of thought and prayer), and to begin to dissolve the idea of the absolute linearity of time. Some scientists are challenging old ideas of what is possible and are devoting incredible intelligence and diligence to consciousness research that meets the most stringent of scientific standards. Leading this effort is the northern California-based Institute of Noetic Sciences (www.noetic.org), which has a website rich in thought-provoking articles, research abstracts, and teleseminars with some of today's leading researchers and philosophers.

While this book is meant to be a practical guide to healing heartache, some readers who would like to see the scientific evidence for the viability of such holistic philosophies that are largely outside of mainstream Western (reductionist, mechanistic, Newtonian) models would do well to do some supplementary reading on quantum physics and research being conducted by the Institute of Noetic Sciences and the Institute of HeartMath, the latter of which is discussed later on.

Outside of Western Europe, indigenous peoples and

their healing traditions have survived to degrees that are generally inversely related to the extent of colonization of their peoples by Western European powers. Despite the myriad cultural variations of indigenous healing philosophies around the globe, traditional healers invariably espouse a view of the human system that is fully integrated and holistic. Biology is one with psychology and both are one with the energy body, often referred to as the soul.

But we don't need to blindly adopt any belief system to know that we are whole, integrated beings. Our direct human experiences tell us that these Western science-asserted separations of mind, body, and this mysterious energy body are not valid. Do we not experience accelerated heart rates and even palpitations when we experience the excitement of a new love? Does our heart not physically ache when we experience great grief? There is certainly something more going on here than what Westerners were taught to believe.

Medical Manifestations of Heartache

Epidemiological studies have shown that people do experience changes in heart activity and sometimes even die from heartache following the loss of a loved one.

A review of epidemiological literature found that mortality from all causes is 50 percent higher among those whose spouses had died when compared with those whose spouses were living.

A study in Finland found that there was a 30 percent increase in the death rate of men in the first six months after the death of their wives and a 20 percent increase thereafter. For women the death rate increased by 20 percent in the first six months and under 10 percent thereafter.

A medical research team at the Central University of Venezuela in Caracas reviewed 102 documented cases of sudden death in people ages thirty-seven to seventy-nine and found that in thirteen cases, the death occurred on the anniversary of a parent's death, apparently related to the resurgence of grief.

The Johns Hopkins University School of Medicine in the United States has also been conducting research on this phenomenon, which the media refers to as "broken heart syndrome." The researchers think that about 2 percent of heart attack patients, roughly thirty thousand people per year in the United States, may actually be experiencing broken heart syndrome. Those experiencing this condition typically feel as though they are having a heart attack and rush to an emergency room, only to find out that there are no blockages in blood flow and a heart attack is ruled out. Researchers are working to identify the hormonal fluctuations that happen in the body during times of grief and learn how those changes affect the heart.

According to research presented at the American Heart Association's Scientific Sessions 2010, the death of a spouse or child can cause elevated heart rate and other potentially harmful heart rhythm changes among the recently bereaved. An article covering this study reports: "Although heart attacks and sudden cardiac death have been shown in some studies to be more common among recently bereaved people, researchers have not been able to explain the cause for this phenomenon, or why the risk appears to dissipate with time."

The quote above represents the current state of scientific understanding regarding the heart's role in love, and it serves as an excellent example of how the physical and social sciences have yet to understand the complexity of the human system. Due to these observations and gaps in understanding, the medical research community is beginning to tie the mind-body systems back together and realize that the individual components cannot be understood in isolation. New fields of psychobiology and psychoneuroimmunology have emerged, and the results of the research are slowly helping to return the scientific view to one of holism.

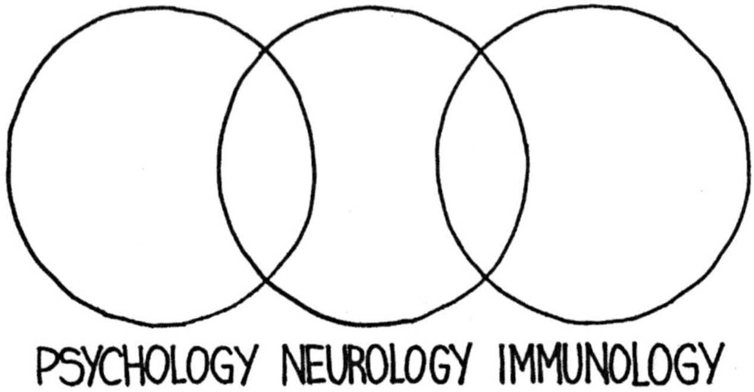

Chapter 5

How Was this Healing Model Developed?

Variations in heart activity resulting from heartache can be fully understood only from holistic perspectives, where mind, body, and spirit are seen as one integrated system. It is clear that heartache is a condition that is not only experienced in the mind and the emotional body, but is also experienced in a measurable and observable way in the physical body. What's more, the physical manifestation of heartache poses real risks to health, and even to life itself, underscoring the critical need for sufferers to actively process their grief and release its effects from the body.

Scientific research often starts with the observation of a phenomenon that is not yet understood. All known aspects of the phenomenon are pieced together, and the scientists then develop a best educated guess about the model at play, a hypothesis. Researchers then carry out a series of experiments to support or invalidate that hypothesis.

The purpose of this book is to share with you the techniques that have worked in my practice. I have laid out a theoretical model for the functioning of the heart that serves as a foundation for this healing work.

What Does "Healing" Mean?

The *Merriam-Webster Dictionary* defines the verb "heal" in the following ways:

a) To make sound or whole
b) To restore to health
c) To cause (an undesirable condition) to be overcome
d) To restore to original purity or integrity

It is easy to define what healing means in the case of a cut or other wound—it is the sealing off of any blood loss, the reforming of tissues, and the final closing of the gap in the skin at the surface, hopefully without a scar! In the case of heartache, we are talking about healing the emotional self. Specifically, we are talking about restoring the healthy functioning of the heart.

As discussed earlier, the emotional function of the heart is reflected in the physical functioning of the heart. A healthy emotional heart is one that feels compassion and empathy, sadness and joy, and one that is open and able to connect with others to form bonds of love, be that love self-focused, social-focused, family-focused, romantic-focused, nature-focused, or spiritual-focused.

To talk of healing in the emotional realms, we are looking to create a sense of peace in the emotional body.

A sense of peace means you feel safe. It means you have an inner sense of self-acceptance, and more ideally, also some self-respect and self-love. When you feel at peace within yourself and your surroundings, you can think of this as an inner coherence among the different systems of your self. When there is peace, all systems of your mind, body, and emotions are synched up—running on the same frequency, resonating with one another. This is known as "coherence."

The Institute of HeartMath, located in the Santa Cruz Mountains of California, conducts research into the role of the heart in our mental, emotional, and physiological lives and provides stress reduction techniques based on its findings. HeartMath recognizes the heart as the master organ of the body and is developing scientific evidence to support this age-old notion.

One of the core tenets of HeartMath is that health and well-being are dependent upon coherence.

HeartMath defines "coherence" in the following manner:

> It [coherence] is the harmonious flow of information, cooperation, and order among the subsystems of a larger system that allows for the emergence of more complex functions. This higher-order cooperation among the physical subsystems, such as the heart, brain, glands, and organs, as well as between the cognitive, emotional, and physical systems, is an important aspect of what we call coherence. It is the rhythm of the heart that sets the beat for the entire system. The heart's rhythmic beat influ-

> ences brain processes that control the autonomic nervous system, cognitive function, and emotions, thus leading us to propose that it is the primary conductor in the system. By changing the rhythm of the heart, system-wide dynamics can be quickly and dramatically changed.

I find the HeartMath description of the role of the heart to be very helpful in working with heartache. Heartache can feel abstract and confusing and overwhelming to people, and so the more models of heart function we have available, the better our ability to understand and navigate healing processes.

Simply put, when we talk about healing heartache, we are talking about making an improvement in your quality of life.

Healing can be instantaneous. It can occur through a single healing event, such as a therapy session, or through an internal realization that shifts the associated feelings. At other times healing is gradual, effected over time through a series of incremental shifts in perspective. The latter case is more common, wherein healing represents a gradual transition of one's emotional, mental, and physical states into ever greater states of balance and harmony. This gradual movement is what people refer to as a healing "path" or "journey."

A healing path or journey can be as long or as short as one chooses for himself or herself. While a healing journey can be guided by forces outside of our conscious awareness, generally the process is aided by holding a mental decision to improve one's quality of life. This is called "holding an intention." Holding an intention for a better experience of one's self and of the world is basically holding a prolonged mental goal. Holding an intention gives the subconscious an instruction and a direction for transforming mental and emotional patterns. When the subconscious is given an instruction, it generally goes to work to find creative and often surprising ways to move you in your desired direction.

You can tailor your own definition of healing based on the specific flavor of your heartache. This definition can also change over time for you. As you reach one plateau, you are often able to see new, higher plateaus to set your next course toward. I have laid out some common goals set by people who are on a healing path from heartache. You can consider these and use them to help structure your own healing goals.

I encourage you to review these goals and identify which ones you would like to work toward before engaging in the techniques provided in this book. Some of the goals may resonate with you, while others may seem like they are too far away to ever be possible. Rest assured: your goals will grow as you grow. You can revisit these goals throughout your healing journey as a way to track your progress and see if you are ready to raise the bar for yourself. This is what I mean about only being able to see a higher plateau once you have reached an intermediate plateau.

The goals are broken out into categories of "how you think about yourself," "how you think about your ex," "how you feel about your ex," and "how you feel in your body." It is helpful to categorize this way because heartache can otherwise feel like drowning in a confused soup of thoughts and feelings.

As you break your thoughts and feelings into categories, you will recognize them as individual components that combine to form your larger experience of heartache. As explained later, thoughts give rise to feelings, so the bulk of healing work will be related to changing how you think, and we will measure progress by checking in on changes in your feelings.

As you review these goals, you will see yourself in them and will identify the main thoughts and feelings that create your own unique heartache blueprint. It will then be easier to dismantle and correct the thoughts and thereby the feelings that come from them.

For the two categories of "thinking" goals, the goals are initially stated in the negative, such as "no longer thinking . . ." Then they are followed by the positive antidotes to the negatives that provide new content for the replacement thoughts. When something is stated in the negative, the mind must first connect with the positive version of the statement before it negates it. For example, if you say to yourself, "I no longer think about my ex," the mind must first identify what it looks, sounds, and feels like to "think about my ex" before it applies the negation. In the process, the mind imagines you thinking about your ex, which then generates a bad feeling. This is not what we want. And so statements must be stated in the positive. Taking the example just provided, you must find some statement that reflects the opposite of thinking about your ex. It takes some practice and creativity, but it is much more effective to find positive statements, such as, "My thoughts are free, independent, and focused on a bright future."

Presented below are several typical goals for recovering from heartache. They are initially written in the "I don't want to . . ." format that we commonly use in a day-to-day speaking. Each such negatively worded goal is then followed by a possible positive version that keeps the mind focused in a healing direction. The positive versions of the goals are indicated by italics.

Goals for how you think about yourself:

- I don't want to beat myself up anymore with guilt and "what ifs." *I accept the past. I put the past in the past, with forgiveness and humility. I embrace the future with openness and excitement.*
- I don't want to think anymore that I am a failure or that something is wrong with me because the relationship ended. *I was only half of the relationship. Like everyone, I am a work in progress, getting better and better over time. I learn from the bumps in the road and continually refine my path toward wholeness.*
- I don't want to think anymore that my self-worth is tied to validation from my ex. *I am my own person with my own worth.*

Goals for how you think about your ex:

- I don't want to think about my ex anymore. I don't want to have obsessive thoughts and behavior. *I give my ex mental and energetic privacy. My energy and focus is clean and self-contained. My peace and happiness are independent of the activity of my ex.*

- I don't want to think that I am missing out. I don't want to think that my ex was "the one" and that we were supposed to be together for life. *My ex was "the one" for the period of time we were together. That is now over. I am learning what I needed to learn and am growing in the ways I needed to grow from this relationship.*

Goals for how you feel about your ex, in order of progression through stages of healing:

- Feeling neutral when thinking of your ex

- Feeling positive when thinking of your ex

- Feeling ready for a friendship with your ex (if appropriate)

- Feeling acceptant of the idea of your ex being with someone else

Goals for how you feel in your body, loosely in order of progression through stages of healing:

- Feeling more connected to the present and the future than the past
- Feeling a lightness in your chest and belly
- Feeling okay with being on your own
- Feeling good about yourself
- Feeling worthy of love
- Feeling open to new romance
- Feeling a sustained flow of self-love

How far you want to take your healing is completely up to you. Since this book will be used by a wide variety of readers, a range of options must be provided. If you are looking for a quick-fix, feel-better solution from your current heartache, then the techniques in the HeartBreak Therapy system will serve you well. If you are looking to break free from a long-standing pattern of recurring heartbreaks, this system will be an excellent starting point to help you gain strength in the short-term and help you to gain insights for next steps to take.

Healing, for those looking to change patterns of recurring heartache, necessitates evolving a strong sense of self, appreciation of self, and love of self. Doing this will not only build emotional resilience, it will often dissolve the bad relationship habits in which you have been engaged.

The first step is examining your role in the pattern and then seeing how a greater sense of self could shift this role and thereby shift the pattern.

What follows is a list of common behaviors to watch out for in unhealthy relationship patterns, followed in italics by an explanation of how greater self-esteem and self-love can dissolve the pattern:

- **Putting your dating partner on a pedestal—assuming the best and ignoring warning signs. "Love is blind."** As you have a stronger sense of self, the gap in respect that you have for yourself and the respect you have for others shrinks. You tend to put people up on pedestals less than before since you yourself have been raised up. You are less desperate for this person to be "the one," and you are able to better see the reality of the person's character and your compatibility.

- **Focusing a lot of mental energy on imagining (fantasizing) how the person you are dating will be your life partner before you really get to know them.** Like the discussion earlier about setting an intention, imagining your dating partner as your spouse sets up the subconscious for deep levels of attachment that can be extremely painful once broken. Don't get too excited. Take it day by day. Keep the jury out for a while. As you have a stronger sense of self, your vision of your future changes from being a vacuum that must be filled by a partner to one that is filled with your own interests. There is less of a void to fill, and you are more selective. You see more clearly. You are more realistic and better attuned to how your dating partner feels about you as a potential longer-term partner.

- **Clinging to your partner, doting, or demanding a lot of your partner's time.** This can suffocate, irritate, and be a turnoff to someone who is just getting to know you. There's something to be said for playing hard to get. "Absence makes the heart grow fonder." Too much sugar can make one sick. As you have a stronger sense of self, your focus shifts from having to "win" your dating partner's favor to seeing what you and this person could co-create that would be mutually beneficial. You are less focused on getting your needs met because more of your needs are already met. Recommended reading: *Love, Freedom, Aloneness: The Koan of Relationships* by Osho.

- **Distrusting, suspicious.** Acting distrusting and suspicious of someone you are dating is a turnoff. It shows your partner that there is a lack of resonance between the two of you. It is the setup for growing distance. Chances are that your dating partner is looking to be

> with someone who is easy to get along with. (Drama is tiresome to those who don't create it.) As you have a stronger sense of self, you have more trust in your instincts about someone's character, and you have a clearer goal of choosing to spend time with people who are honest and trustworthy. You put the days of deceitful partners in the past, where they belong. As you enter a new dating situation, you trust that you are breaking new ground and creating a healthy relationship.

A stronger sense of self heals most relationship issues either by removing the cause of the issue or, in the case of a true incompatibility or deceit, dissolving the relationship without a large impact to the self. Developing this kind of emotional resilience to the fullest extent means getting good with being with yourself—getting good with not having a partner and getting good with being alone.

Life does not guarantee a healthy, loving, long-term romantic partnership to every person. Sure, you can optimize your chances, but there is no guarantee. Getting good with being on your own is a huge goal to work toward and a powerful one to achieve. Being good with being alone is an absolutely necessary precursor to moving into a relationship without any sense of need or desperation. It is only from such a baseline emotional state that you can move into a relationship out of pure choice, with both of you only adding to, and not detracting from, one another's lives. It is an ideal state from which to create a true, beautiful form of synergistic love, companionship, and co-nurturing.

Being in a relationship with someone to get your needs met can feel good when a relationship is running smoothly, but as things break down, all of your weaknesses, shadows, and fears rise to the surface. For someone who would otherwise be miserable as a single person, being "happy" because they are in a relationship is simply retarding their emotional growth until such time they are faced with being alone once again and forced to deal with the reality of the human condition.

Conversely, after developing a higher level of emotional maturity and emotional intelligence, one can enter into a relationship out of choice instead of out of need. Entering a relationship in such a way offers an incredible freedom to fully express joy without fear, doubt, or self-consciousness. This is not to say that the two individuals in a relationship will remain emotionally independent. The very nature of love is such that it changes us. It is common for those who come together out of pure choice to grow into an interwoven codependency. Even this is then part of the choice of coming together. Two choose to meld into one. This is quite different from two who feel empty when alone and who cling to one another in a desperate attempt to feel whole.

This path of being okay with being on one's own is not for everyone. Not everyone is ready for it. Most people just want to feel good and are looking for the shortest and quickest path to get there. It is my job to lay out some options for you, but the choice is ultimately yours.

> The most terrifying thing is to accept oneself completely.
>
> —*Carl Gustav Jung*

If getting good with being alone feels like too much for you, consider it again once you have read the chapter of this book called "The Three Kinds of Love." This chapter explains how self-love is only one of three kinds of love that our heart needs to be fully and healthily functioning. The chapter will show you how you can get your needs for the other two kinds of love met without being in a romantic relationship, thereby making the above-described path much more approachable.

A Healing Model

Since modern science cannot explain what is happening during heartache, and modern psychology does not have much to offer for the processing and release of grief, I turn to well-established holistic perspectives, such as the concept of the energy body and the heart chakra, as described earlier. A fully developed healing model needs to first identify how a healthy heart functions, and then explain what happens when we experience a heartache-inducing loss.

I developed a model that:

- Is consistent with other holistic healing models in that it is rooted in love, forgiveness, and compassion, for both one's self and for others
- Embraces all of the experiences that life brings us, both the joyful and the painful
- Emphasizes love as the life-force of the universe
- Acknowledges that heartache is a natural function of the heart, that having heartache is one of the natural oscillations of life as a human being, and that these painful swings should never be associated with guilt, shame, or a sense of failure
- Makes it not only safe and okay to open our hearts to love, but critically important to do so in order to be fully human
- Embraces the fact that heartache can and will happen and that the experience itself is a teacher that aids us in our spiritual growth and learning

- Embraces the notion that thought is energy and that our own thoughts direct our own energy
- Emphasizes the importance of loving one's self at least as much as we allow ourselves to love anyone or anything external to us

The Model of Heart Function

When we lose a loved one, either through death or breakup, our heart registers the break of an energetic love connection with another being, and thus becomes destabilized.

The heart can be thought of as a love transceiver—acting as both the transmitter of our love going out to others and the receiver of love from others. When the flow of love is broken—either love outflow or inflow—we experience heartache.

Deaths and breakups are typically experienced as a loss of a source (inflow) of love that the departed represented to us, as well as a loss of an object of our love (outflow). So in the same event, we have lost both the source of our inflow and the destination of our outflow of love. There is no love coming in, and love being generated in the heart has nowhere to go. The flow has been stopped and the heart goes into a state of shock.

Most often during heartache, the sufferer tends to think of the love that has been taken away; the focus is upon the cutting off of the inflow of love. Examining heart function from this inflow perspective, falling in love with someone means opening our hearts and allowing love to flow into us from that person. It is when that inward flow of love from an external source is suddenly stopped that we feel the pain.

When the flow of love we have come to expect and often depend upon is removed, it is like an energy supply has been shut off and our system is knocked out of balance. It's an energetic blackout in our system. We come to rely on the love of a partner as a table relies on four legs for its stability. When one of the legs is removed, the table is destabilized.

Fortunately, we are not tables. We are dynamic, adaptable beings, who like all living systems are constantly seeking a return to balance, health, and functionality, what biologists term "homeostasis." It is our natural response to eventually rebalance ourselves.

Rebalancing after a loss of love inflow is accomplished in various ways. Some involve keeping the heart open to receiving love, some involve closing the heart for a time and then reopening it, and others involve closing the heart for the long-term.

Keeping the heart open is generally healthier on all levels than any closed-heart responses, although some open-hearted options are healthier than others. The ideal response is to keep the heart open and to find that source of love in one's self. Establishing or reestablishing a connection with one's own self-love can be accomplished through self-care, self-nurturing, and self-reflection.

A less ideal open-hearted response is to have a rebound relationship and jump immediately to find someone else who will fill that role as a source of love. Jumping to a new relationship doesn't allow for a full experiencing of the emotions of the grief process and all of the personal growth and learning that comes with that journey.

While healthy responses allow for a recovery, unhealthy responses only serve to memorialize the pain in the psyche and personality of the individual. When one does not engage in a healthy, self-love-based recovery, there are many unfortunate and unhealthy paths that are often taken, including:

- Closing the heart and reducing the expectation of love through feelings of hopelessness or of not deserving love
- Closing off to allowing any new external sources of love flow into the heart through feeling jaded, hopeless, or undeserving
- Trying to lessen the pain through distractions or obsessions, such as work, shopping, travel, sports, movies, and hobbies
- Numbing the pain through addictions, such as food, alcohol, and drugs

Numbing the pain for a while will make it worse when you finally feel it.

—J.K. Rowling

Experiencing heartache and recovering on your own is one of the most spiritual experiences you can have. The process of reconnecting to your self-love can be beautiful and ecstatic. Those first days of moving beyond the heartache are magical. Suddenly one day you are waking up happy, feeling healthfully detached from the previous relationship, and having that zest for life once again. It is the archetypal journey from separateness back to oneness.

And so this is the model of healing we use in this book. The collection of techniques provided in *Heart-*

Break Therapy is designed primarily to help you cultivate a healthy, sustainable flow of self-love.

Along with the energetic and emotional shifts that occur from heartache, there are the mental interpretations that our minds make in response to the breakup. It is all too common for us to judge a breakup as a failure or a rejection and to then interpret the event as a reflection of our self-worth, our attractiveness, or our ability to be a part of a successful relationship. Since our beliefs about ourselves and the world determine the thoughts that we have, and since our thoughts direct our energy (and love flow), the techniques in this book address unhealthy beliefs and thoughts, thereby redirecting the flow of love into healthy, sustainable, and self-empowering directions. Through correcting mental misinterpretations of events in your life, the techniques in this system help you to shift your mental chatter from self-loathing to self-loving and help to bring that flow of love back home to you, where it belongs.

Chapter 6

Harvesting the Benefits of Heartache

The question is often asked, "What is a healthy grieving timeframe?" Most people agree that it is normal and healthy to experience the emotions associated with loss, be it from a death or through a separation. But how long is long enough? At what point does the grieving go on for too long? There is no consensus. This is something you have to decide for yourself.

Let's consider the options:

- If you enjoy the pain, then you'll keep it around.
- If you benefit from the pain, then you'll also likely keep it around.
- If you have something to learn from the pain, it's best that you focus upon identifying the lesson and learning it; otherwise, you are likely to repeat your patterns that led you to this place and be faced with similar heartache once again.

If after serious introspection you are clear that you have nothing to learn from the pain, then you are likely ready to move on from this emotional state as soon as possible.

Unconscious Benefits of Heartache

Let's look more closely at the possibility that you may be receiving benefit from your heartache. Unconscious motivations to stay in heartache may be blocking you from achieving your conscious goal of feeling better. It is worth spending some time examining this possibility and either dealing with it or ruling it out. Here are some possible benefits from heartache to consider:

- If you are a writer or an artist, emotional pain may bring you inspiration and add depth to your work.
- If heartache brings you closer to friends and family through their sympathies and empathies, then this is a benefit to you.
- If your emotional life is already one of continuous cycles of highs and lows, then emotional pain through heartache may be a way of subconsciously creating the downswing phase of this already established pattern. You may have a belief that lasting peace and happiness is not achievable. The subconscious can then draw you into situations that will end the happy phases and bring you back into emotional upset. The subconscious can do this by drawing you into relationships that are doomed from

the beginning, or can sabotage relationships that are working well. If such a pattern is presenting, it is critical to examine your beliefs around your ability to have lasting happiness, love and fulfillment. Also check for any beliefs that you do not deserve to be loved, to be happy and to be fulfilled. Working with a hypnotherapist can help you to quickly identify any such root causes.

- If you are normally extroverted, active, and happy, and don't take much quiet time for introspection and personal development, then the down time heartache provides may serve as that contrasting experience that brings balance and a more rounded human experience. As mentioned earlier, all systems seek balance—if you go too high for too long, you are likely to crash. If your life is constantly exploding outward, your system will find a way to implode now and then.

You may be able to find other benefits you are reaping from being in a state of heartache. It is critical that you ask yourself what benefits there may be to your heartache so that you can identify them and make any needed adjustments to your life.

If heartache is bringing you balance, how can you manage your life differently so that your system doesn't seek to crash to find that balance?

If you have unidentified benefits to your pain, these

can act as saboteurs and hold you back when you are trying to move on. Meditating and journaling on these questions are great ways to extract inner wisdom and find the answers so you can move on.

Heartache as Teacher

If you find that heartache causes you to look inward and opens a window to accelerated personal growth and development, then you are on the right track. By embracing life's trials with humility, honesty, and a sincere desire to learn and evolve, you will move through its challenges with much more ease.

Often the higher purpose of the most difficult challenges and losses in life is to teach you something—to force you to grow in areas where you have resisted earlier warnings and chosen not to grow voluntarily. From this perspective, you can view your heartache as your teacher, showing you where you need the most growth at this moment in your life.

Consider some of the common lessons that heartache seeks to teach and see if they apply to you:

- Do you need to be a better judge of character with respect to romantic partners?
- Do you need to act on warning signs instead of ignoring them?
- Do you need to pay more attention to body language and sensing when someone is not being honest with you?
- Do you need to put more effort into communication and make fewer assumptions about what a partner is thinking or feeling?
- Do you need to be more honest in your relationships and with yourself?
- Are you repeating old patterns from your own past relationships?
- Are you repeating the relationship patterns of your parents?
- Do you need to love yourself more?

Once you have identified something you need to learn, how do you proceed? First, you need to own the lesson(s). Secondly, you need to commit to making the learning happen. This essentially makes a pact with the part of you that wants you to learn. It says, "If I agree to learn this, then you agree to release me from this pain." This can be done through a clear mental or verbal conversation with yourself, stating strongly, "I need to learn ______, and I commit to learning this from this day forward."

Make any other commitments to yourself that seem to make sense given the topic at hand. Suggestions for such additional commitments are provided here for the above-listed lessons, in the same order:

- "I am only interested in dating someone who [insert quality that was missing from your partner]."
- "From now on, I pay attention to warning signs in my relationships. I step back, evaluate the risk, and act appropriately."
- "Actions speak louder than words. I pay attention to my partner's actions and body language and check for alignment with their words."
- "I communicate clearly and completely. I make no assumptions."
- "Honesty is integrity. I am open and honest with my partner. I am honest with myself."
- "I release myself from the relationship patterns of my past and I start anew."
- "I am my own person. I dissolve any unhealthy patterns from my parents. My life is open, and I am free to make my own choices. I claim my freedom, my independence, and I define healthy relationships on my terms."

- "I love myself more than anyone else. My self-love is my foundation."

The Critical Importance of Self-Love

The last statement in the list above, about self-love, is absolutely critical to consider. It is fundamental to making effective use of the statements provided higher up in the list. Without a healthy flow of self-love, none of the earlier statements have much power behind them. But with a strong sense of self-love, they can be strong, directive, commanding, and transformative.

For many people with recurring patterns of relationship challenges, a lack of self-love is their critical issue. The key issue here is that like attracts like. Whatever your ability to love yourself may be, you are most likely to feel comfortable with someone whose love for you matches the level or quality of love that you have for yourself.

It is natural to reject someone who does not treat you as well as you treat yourself because in such a situation you'll have an inherent sense that you deserve to be treated better. But with a lack of self-love, we can have a fear of being alone, and so we can hold onto a relationship, even if it isn't good for us. This then creates a conflict in the relationship because you are demanding better of your partner, your partner is not providing, yet you stay involved. Instead of releasing both of you to your own lives, the lack of self-love creates a desperate and destructive love addiction. When self-love is lacking, bad love is better than no love at all. Being in a relationship with someone who treats you poorly can result in continual disappointment, frustration, conflict, and either prolonged unhappiness or, finally, a breakup.

The reverse is also true. While you may, for a period of time, attract someone who sees you in a more loving light than you see yourself, the relationship is not likely to last because you will have an inherent sense that you do not deserve the excessive flow of love you are receiving. This situation leads to suspicion as to the authenticity of your partner's affection, and it causes you to doubt and sabotage the relationship through being dishonest, hurtful, unreliable, or playing games in order to feel like you are in power. You may even convince yourself that your partner is going to leave you, and so you leave him or her first because it is always easier to dump someone than to get dumped.

Sabotage can be seen a subconscious effort to make your partner reduce his or her expressions of love down to a level that you think you deserve. If your level of self-love is low, then you feel more comfortable with a certain degree of conflict and drama than you do with someone who treats you like a god or goddess. The instinct to sabotage something good is like the sickening feeling you can get from a dessert that is too sweet and too rich. Sabotage is like the black coffee we drink alongside the dessert to take the sweetness down a notch. In a sickly sweet relationship, the love we are getting is too sweet, too rich for our soured heart; therefore, we add some bitterness to the relationship to make it an accurate reflection of what we know love to be, based on our past experiences of love. Some of the things we are unconsciously saying to our partner when we are sabotaging are: "Get away from me!" "Don't be so nice to me!" "When are you going to turn on me?"

Generally, sabotage ends in a breakup, which either you initiate (because you have spun yourself into such an obsessive paranoia that it makes you crazy and you can't handle not knowing the truth) or your partner initiates (because he or she is not willing to tolerate the drama you continue to bring to the table).

You will reject those who love you less than you love yourself, and you will sabotage those who love you more, leaving you only having a chance at a relationship with people who love you around the same degree as you love yourself. This is partly why loving yourself first, and loving yourself as much as possible, is absolutely critical to maximizing your chances of a successful, lasting relationship.

And for another perspective, Barbara De Angelis, an American researcher on relationships and personal growth says, "If you aren't good at loving yourself, you will have a difficult time loving anyone, since you'll resent the time and energy you give another person that you aren't even giving to yourself."

If you are like most people, the nature of your self-love is a product of how you were loved as a child. The vast majority of emotional issues that adults face are due to either a lack of parental love or the misdirected expression of that love. How to heal this is beyond the scope of this book, but it can be achieved over a period of time with determination and a commitment to a better life. There are many therapists, workshops, books, spiritual paths, and self-development programs that can aid you in such a healing journey. I personally recommend hypnotherapy as a starting point, since it is the most direct form of emotional healing I know of.

I don't like myself, I'm crazy about myself.

—Mae West

How Long Is Long Enough?

If you have sincerely and honestly examined and exhausted all opportunities for growing from the experience of heartache and have determined that it has no useful role in your life, what other benefits are there in keeping it around?

Answering this question of "how long is enough?" also relates to your personal philosophy. If you come from a family, culture, or religion that places a huge importance on being in a relationship by a certain age and would have you feeling guilty or like a failure for a breakup, then you would likely feel inclined to draw out the misery for a longer period of time. However, if you are free from such external programming, then you have a greater chance of seeing life as a more fluid and open system that holds more space for adventure, learning, and growth. Let's explore this latter perspective.

To fully embrace life for all that it has to offer, and to make the best of our lives, it is a formidable goal to not personalize events and experiences. Personalizing an event means making the event personal, allowing it to affect our self-image. If someone yells at you, you have the choice of either feeling bad about yourself, lashing out and getting angry, or not being affected at all and simply noting that the person in front of you is having an emotional outburst. The latter approach is more emotionally healthy and mature than the former. You are better able to move through the situation with compassion and loving-kindness for the person having the difficult emotion. You are able to clearly see that the one who is suffering is the one in front of you, and you are able to live the instruction brought by many a wise master of "love your enemy."

To cleanly and smoothly navigate this human reality, we must realize that who we are is simply consciousness. That is, our true essence is not our mind or our thoughts or our emotions, since they are all transient; they have no consistency over time. Rather, our soul is a constant awareness within us that observes the emotions and thoughts passing through our experience. Except for this awareness, nothing else in our lives is constant. So how can any of those constantly fluctuating factors "be" us?

When you are depressed, you are not inherently a depressed being. You are merely temporarily having the experience of depression. Even within the depression there exists the awareness that you are down, off-track, misaligned. That part of you that wants you to get to a balanced and joyous state of being is your soul's perspective—the continuity of awareness that transcends all experience.

When we see that a conscious observer is all that we are, we can see that we are not our thoughts, we are not our emotions, we are not our bodies, our jobs, our race, our sexuality, or our relationships. When we lose a job, a relationship, or even a limb, we have not lost a core part of ourselves—we have not lost any part of the constant observer. (A deeper exploration into this concept is provided in Michael Singer's book, *The Untethered Soul.*)

If one is able to fully adopt this philosophy, the loss of a relationship has much less intensity since the individual can see herself (the observer) as fully intact, and the only challenge is to adjust to a change in external conditions. Under this philosophy, you are complete before your relationship, you are complete within the relationship (independent of your partner), and you emerge from the relationship still complete. The relationship was simply an experience that had a beginning and an end.

Since consciousness seeks to learn and to grow, and learning and growing are best done through direct experience, a full embodiment of this philosophy would allow one to leave a relationship with a sense of inner peace and calm, as well as a sense of gratitude for the experience of the relationship, regardless of what transpired.

In summary, the reason we experience pain from a breakup is because we have a flawed sense of our own identity. We have "over-identified" with external factors, meaning that we have considered external factors to be actual extensions of who we are, rather than considered them as experiences we are having. There is no need to stay in the pain, and it is desirable to return to a healthy perspective of one's own wholeness as soon as one is able.

If it is possible to be in a state of such clear self-awareness, self-love, and self-acceptance that you can leave a relationship with no pain and no heartache, would that be healthy? Few are dedicated enough to this path to actually achieve this state of being, but those who do, or who at least come close, are considered to be highly functioning, emotionally and psychologically healthy, and are leading happy and productive lives. Indeed there is a growing branch of modern psychotherapy that is considering Buddhist philosophy as a framework for helping people to reframe their realities to healthier perspectives.

I have helped people out of their heartache at several points along the post-loss timeline. And I have known people who were in heartache who didn't feel ready to move on from their pain. The answer about a healthy grieving timeframe lies only within you. If you are ready to move on, then the time is right for you.

You may ask yourself, "What would life be like if I could heal instantly from a shift in external circumstances and immediately return to an open, loving, playful, and trusting state of being?" If your answer is a positive one, then you can expect to benefit greatly from the exercises in this book.

In summary, there are two key points to consider as you complete this chapter; these are summarized below.

1. To be an emotionally healthy human being, you need to make sure you are learning from your experiences. If you feel you need pain to learn, then accept the pain and commit to self-reflection, learning, and growing amidst the discomfort. If you are someone who learns in a gentler manner, through correcting your course as you go by, observing more subtle cues about what works and what doesn't, then you are probably not as well adapted to experiencing intense emotions, and you may choose to minimize your heartache if given the tools. I am hoping this book will help you to make that choice.
2. Your recovery from heartache should be a healthy one, that is, through reconnecting

to your own self-love. If you can achieve this quickly, then you are successful in making this experience one of personal growth and evolution. Learning to connect to your own self-love will aid you in every area of your life, and will make the trials that are inherent to human existence much more bearable.

Chapter 7

Hypnotherapy and Neuro-Linguistic Programming

It has been said that when we come into this world nobody gives us an owner's manual for our mind and emotions.

How are we supposed to live a psychologically and emotionally healthy life if nobody teaches us how to? What tools are there to manage these aspects of ourselves? Isn't there a better way than being at the mercy of the fear, the negative self-talk, and the old limiting beliefs of our parents that seem to control us from some powerful place deep within? And why do our efforts to overcome these old patterns often feel in vain?

Many are not even aware that it is possible to change these aspects of one's self, let alone to name a tool for doing so. Most people surrender to their conditioning, with an attitude of "that's just how I am." Thus they sadly give up on themselves and accept a sentence of being prisoner to a life founded on beliefs they had no say in in the first place. Life then becomes one big compromise, and everyone who interacts with such people must also compromise. It's not a fair outcome for anyone involved when we surrender to negative programming.

Hypnotherapy and Neuro-Linguistic Programming (NLP) are two healing modalities that, when studied in conjunction with one another, combine to form what can be considered an owner's manual for the mind and emotions. Since the purpose of this book is to provide you with long-lasting emotional healing at the subconscious level, and since this book and accompanying audio use hypnotherapy and NLP to effect this healing, let's explore the concepts of the conscious mind, subconscious mind, and how these healing techniques work.

A Tale of Two Minds

Most people think that they are their conscious mind and that the subconscious is some out-of-control programming to which we have no access. We often speak from the perspective of the conscious mind, saying things like: "I was asleep," "I had this dream," "I keep having these thoughts," "This voice in my head," "This image just came to me." But this is a limited perspective of the self. The conscious mind is only one part of our consciousness, of our selves.

By thinking that we are our conscious minds, it is like the paint on a house thinking that it is the house. The paint can't see the structure that supports it and gives it shape. The conscious mind is like the paint—the outer layer of our consciousness that interfaces with the world—while the subconscious is like the blueprint designs, the foundation, the frame, and the actual walls, floors, and roof.

You say, "I was asleep," but while you were asleep, your subconscious mind was awake and active.

You say, "I had this dream," but while you were "having" a dream, your subconscious mind was orchestrating the entire virtual reality that you experienced as a dream.

You say, "I keep having these thoughts," but the thoughts that you keep having and the voice you keep hearing are being spoken to you from your subconscious mind.

You say, "This image just came to me," but the image that just came to you was presented to you from your subconscious mind.

As you can see, there is a whole other you below the

surface that is deep, wise, creative, metaphoric, mystical, and mysterious. That is the subconscious mind. So who are you, really?

If you are not limited to your conscious mind, you are something much, much more. You are something very creative, very powerful, and very mysterious. This is where the exploration of hypnosis begins to open up large philosophical and spiritual questions about the nature of consciousness. This is where a self-hypnosis or meditation practice can spark a curiosity about one's inner self and can deepen one's sense of self-appreciation and, hopefully, self-love.

There is a beautiful mystery inside of you, awaiting your discovery. There is another part of you that you can engage in conversation: an inner counsel, an inner sage.

> Knowing others is intelligence; knowing yourself is true wisdom. Mastering others is strength; mastering yourself is true power.
>
> —*Author Unknown*

The other part of the mind is the conscious mind. The conscious mind is the part of you that is active when you are awake, engaged, walking down the street, having a conversation, making a shopping list, and preparing meals. The conscious mind is often referred to as the "critical factor," meaning it is the part of the mind that thinks critically. The conscious mind filters information for validity, deciding what is reasonable and realistic and what is not.

The conscious mind judges and analyzes. The filtering, judging, and analysis is done based on existing beliefs about ourselves and the world. The critical factor helps us to discern rational from irrational in the waking world. The conscious mind is the decision maker.

Together, the subconscious and conscious minds form your stream of consciousness—the never-ending flow of thoughts that occur from moment to moment, ever changing. The totality of your consciousness is a mixture of conscious choices and unconscious reactions. Attractions and repulsions combine to form tastes, opinions, and preferences. Some of these preferences are formed by logic and reasoning (conscious mind), while others come from somewhere inside of us as an instinct (subconscious mind).

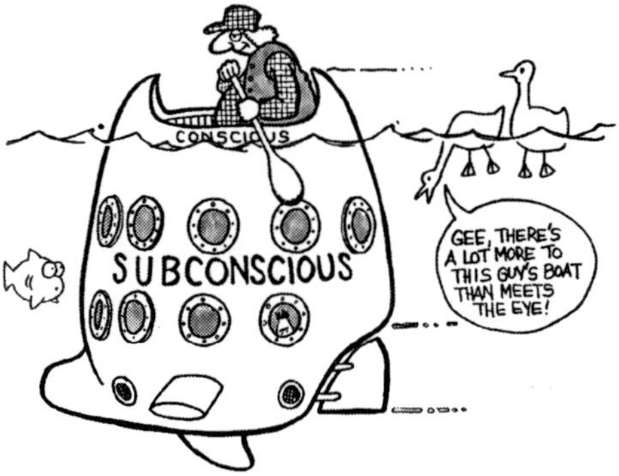

Why do we have two minds? The best we can do at this time is to describe the characteristics of the two minds. We have some ideas about how they work and complement one another, but the "why" is one of the fascinating mysteries that keep us asking questions and seeking greater and deeper truths.

Let's look at the two minds from an evolutionary standpoint. We are part of the animal kingdom. Like all mammals, we are under the care of our parents until we reach sexual maturity, at which point we branch out on our own, find a mate, and start our adult lives.

This prepubescent period of being under the care of our parents is necessarily a period of rapid learning. Within a few years of our birth, we must learn to feed, walk, run, understand and speak language, hunt and gather food, evade predators and other threats, and find or construct shelter. It is paramount to our survival that we learn as quickly as we can.

Once that learning period is over, life is about putting those lessons into action so we can survive in the world and protect our own young. Learning is not a priority for the adult.

If you were the genius creator/nature, how would you design a mind to meet both needs? How would you design a mind that accomplishes both rapid learning in one phase of life and ease of implementation in another phase?

You can see the challenge of the situation. Having two types of software running at the same time can consume too many resources and can make for a cluttered situation. What about having a system whereby one processor is turned off while the other one is running? What about having one turned on while waking and the other turned on while sleeping? What about having the learning part of the mind develop first in the womb, while the other part develops only later during puberty, leaving us with two minds? All of these models seem to be at play with our current conscious-subconscious mind system.

When we are awake (conscious), the subconscious mind is "resting" outside of our awareness. Likewise, when the subconscious is active, the conscious mind is at rest (we don't question the reality our dreams while we are in them – it is only after we wake and regain our conscious faculty that we see how unrealistic they are). Studies on how we learn have shown that while we go through the motions of learning while we are awake, it is during our sleep that the information is consolidated and the learning process is completed. The conscious mind takes information in, and it is held there until sleep time, where the information is turned over to the subconscious for processing and storage. So we see here the role of the subconscious as the learner of skills.

Likewise, the free-form, creative, and metaphoric nature of the subconscious doesn't necessarily lend itself to performing practical tasks in linear time and physical reality. That is left to the conscious mind, to actively weigh variables and make decisions. The subconscious is always present in the background as the great database of memory and experience that we continually access, but what we perceive as our waking "thought process" is generally the linear stream of consciousness of the conscious mind.

What about the idea mentioned earlier of having one part of the mind develop early in life and then having another part develop later? We can see that this also occurs in the development of the human mind.

From examining the characteristics of the conscious and subconscious minds, we can see that children lack a well-developed conscious mind and live largely from the subconscious. This is evidenced by the loose grip on ordinary reality that children have. Children have imaginary friends that they perceive to be real, have fantasies of super powers that they learned about from books or movies, believe the wildest of stories that other people tell, are highly creative, and in general have blurred boundaries between reality and fiction. Children easily learn to speak other languages, to ride a bicycle, or to swim, and they largely do these without the fear that would be experienced by most adults attempting to undertake the same challenges. All of these attributes are characteristic of the subconscious mind.

When children reach adolescence, they begin to question what they are told, answer back to parents and teachers, and generally start thinking for themselves. There is a strong instinct to develop their own interests and to "leave the nest," which shows up as diverging from the parents and the educational system that has directed their lives up until that point.

This age-old instinct is evolutionarily critical. The desire for independence in the world that comes along with sexual maturity at age twelve to fourteen is a necessary urge so that young members of a species can begin their own families and keep their genetic line moving forward.

The development of the conscious mind coincides with this transition. The attributes of the conscious mind of filtering, analyzing, judging, and rejecting certain pieces of information are being developed during this time, often to the dismay of the parents and teachers trying to do the "right thing" for the youth.

And so we have the evolutionary model of our mind: the first years of life are run mostly from the subconscious in a state of wide open, rapid learning, and from puberty on we tend to be more rigid in our ideas, learning is more difficult, and whatever we learned from childhood tends to be "locked in." This is exactly why most people's emotional baggage dates back to childhood.

Many adults, particularly males, are used to communicating their desires through anger and displays of strength. Consider how males compete for females in nature—puffing up of chests, charging at one another ending in a clash of antlers, flashing colors, doing a fancy dance.

When this approach to communication is applied to child rearing, with anger and threats being directed toward a child, emotional damage to the child typically results. The child, not understanding the parent's psychology or background, typically assumes that it did something wrong and interprets the "attack" by the parent as a message of being unworthy or unlovable. Self-esteem is damaged at the core. In those cases where the child does happen to have a well-developed sense of self and where the self-esteem is generally intact, the parental outbursts are still usually interpreted into a belief that the world is unsafe and that people who love you cannot be relied upon to stick around.

Likewise, parents who are emotionally disconnected or unexpressive, depressed, or under a lot of stress tend to create an uneasy environment and tend not to express the gentle, supportive love that a child needs to develop a healthy mind and balanced emotions. In most cases, parents' inappropriate behaviors result in self-loathing and life-fearing perspectives in the child's mind. These perspectives solidify into beliefs, which are locked into place by puberty, to create a life of emotional and mental imbalance. Once the conscious mind has developed, it is like a hard coating overlying the soft subconscious. Unlearning those early life interpretations of ourselves and our world then becomes very difficult.

Hypnotherapy

Hypnotherapy involves relaxing the mind into a state of consciousness similar to meditation and then using words and the imagination to reprogram our beliefs that form the basis of our psychology and our behavior.

Hypnotherapy is therapy conducted in the state of hypnosis, which is a natural state that we all go into every day. Hypnosis is a state of mind between waking and sleeping where our attention is highly focused. We all pass through hypnotic states as we fall asleep and as we wake up.

Most of us also go into a state of hypnosis within

about sixty seconds of watching television. Think about what it is like when you are watching an intense moment in a movie: your entire attention is upon what is happening within the bounds of the screen. You are not aware of the walls, ceiling, or floor of your living room. Your heart is racing and you are sharing the emotions of the protagonist. Perhaps someone in the room is asking you a question, but your mind is so engrossed in the film that you don't hear them. In that moment, a part of your consciousness believes that what is happening in the movie is real, and you are disconnected from ordinary reality.

This is what happens in a hypnotherapy session. Healing scenarios are co-created by the hypnotherapist and the client, and the client experiences the healing holographically—that is, with all of the senses in a way that is perceived to be real and three dimensional. Just like in the movie where the protagonist is running down an alley to escape his pursuer, you experience the three dimensionality of that chase.

Another state of consciousness similar to hypnosis is that of dreaming. When you are dreaming, you do not question the wild and unrealistic nature of what is occurring. Likewise, in hypnosis, all things are possible, and we are able to bypass the conscious mind/rational mind/critical factor.

Going into the state of hypnosis allows us to employ the power of the imagination to create situations that are perceived as being real. The subconscious accepts these created scenarios as being just as real as the memories from childhood. This allows us to achieve great emotional healing.

If we have negative or limiting beliefs that were put into place due to some negative past experiences, then attempts at bringing positive change can be discarded by the conscious mind before making it through to the subconscious. This is why we want to relax the conscious mind out of the way. Hypnosis relaxes the conscious mind so that we have more direct access to the subconscious mind and to the ideas stored within.

In summary, we want to access our subconscious mind because that is where we store our beliefs and assumptions about ourselves and the world. Most of our emotional problems are stored in the subconscious as beliefs based on misguided interpretations of past experiences. In hypnosis, the protective filter of the conscious mind is reduced or removed, allowing our normally rigid beliefs to become soft and malleable. This means that the imagination, discussed above, can be used to create new realities. Since in hypnosis the conscious mind is reduced or removed, the subconscious accepts these new realities created in hypnosis, and a new belief or perspective is then in place. These new realities, when strategically created to contrast existing dysfunctional beliefs, can neutralize the old belief and relieve the related emotional dysfunction and behavioral patterns.

Neuro-Linguistic Programming

Neuro-Linguistic programming, or NLP, is a modality that was developed through the study of therapy sessions conducted by three well-known and successful American-based therapists, including the twentieth century's most famous hypnotherapist, Milton Erickson.

NLP is a set of guided techniques involving language and the imagination aimed at recoding how the mind stores and interprets information. NLP is a rapid way to neutralize emotional charges on memories, dissolve fears and phobias, and change beliefs that are limiting to ones that are positive and empowering. NLP is largely conducted with the eyes closed, which naturally creates a very light trance, but it does not involve the client going into a full bypass of the critical mind. The willing participation of the client in the techniques is considered enough to reprogram the subconscious.

I personally see hypnotherapy as the mystical mother of the cold and rational NLP child. While NLP can be very effective, it lacks the sense of magic and mystery that comes with going into hypnosis and experiencing deeper and mystical aspects of the self. And while hypnotherapy is beautiful and mystical, it can be difficult to grasp and obscure to implement to the more logical and rational-minded among us. Where studying NLP can be a great path for reaching inside to "fix" things that are out of place, I feel that engaging in hypnotherapy is in essence a spiritual path, where increasingly magical inner layers of self are revealed.

The study of both modalities together creates a wonderful perspective and skill set for understanding and healing ourselves and for making our lives more peaceful, interesting, and fulfilling. Understand hypnotherapy and NLP and you can understand the majority of the questions we have about human nature.

Hypnotherapy and NLP are powerful and effective, yet they remain largely unknown to the general public. As with many non-mainstream modalities, there is a lack of documentation and academic or institutional attention given to hypnotherapy and NLP. And yet those who practice them find that they often achieve rapid and lasting shifts in emotional, psychological, and medical conditions with none of the side effects associated with pharmaceuticals and at a fraction of the cost and time associated with the commonly used institutions of psychotherapy and modern medicine.

I see these techniques as being shamanic in their nature. Like shamans, hypnotherapists and NLP practitioners work in their local communities, they work with people one-on-one, they achieve levels of healing in single sessions that most Westerners would call "miracles," and they do not require much in the way of time, money, or resources. Yet exactly how they do what they do remains, to most people, a mystery. While hypnotherapy and NLP are not at all mysterious in how they are used, they are mysterious in terms of how and why they work.

Hypnotherapy and NLP are focused on what actually works. They are all about change and changing now. I can't count how many clients have come to me after being in psychotherapy for several years with only limited results, and in their first session with hypnotherapy and NLP, they achieved the result they had been seeking for so long. Most people find that psychotherapy is a wonderful process for understanding one's emotional patterns but that it falls short of actually changing those patterns.

Hypnotherapy and NLP are not only useful for treating others in a therapeutic setting—they are also very powerful self-development tools. Studying hypnotherapy and NLP can provide incredible insight on how to consciously choose what you believe, think, and feel, instead of being a helpless victim of the belief patterns, thought patterns, and emotional patterns instilled throughout your upbringing.

These healing techniques allow individuals to resolve their own emotional issues from the past and to move forward in life in a clear and conscious manner with a framework that fosters a healthy interpretation of life's circumstances. This is in contrast to moving through life with a more negative interpretation of life's circumstances, which can result in the adoption of limiting beliefs, which in turn reduce one's openness to love, trust, joy, and the ability to have a fulfilling life.

All people can benefit from understanding how to manage their own beliefs, thoughts, and emotions and how to retrain themselves to be healthier, more whole human beings.

To qualify as humans,
we must partake in humanitarian acts.

—José Silva, founder of The Silva Method

Chapter 8

Reframing

Many processes in this book are about reframing situations. The perspective on any situation in one's life depends on how it is framed. Developing the ability to reframe situations at will allows one to be an empowered chooser of one's experience of life.

What does reframing mean? Given a certain situation, reframing means consciously choosing what perspective to take on it and what parts to focus upon. For instance, a photographer can take a thousand different photographs of the same subject. As he looks through the camera's viewfinder, the photographer chooses how to frame the subject. He chooses what is included in the frame, what is excluded, what is in focus, and what is out of focus. He frames the photo and then makes the image of his choosing.

Reframing is taking an existing situation and looking at it differently by focusing upon or emphasizing different parts, changing the perspective. A classic application of this is to "look for the silver lining" of a storm cloud, which is an excellent tool optimists use. Circumstances of lack or loss always offer an opportunity for growth and learning.

There are several truisms in our language that capture this concept: Every end is a new beginning. As one door closes, another opens. The glass is half full, not half empty. These are all reframes used to uplift and encourage those feeling beaten down by difficult circumstances. Simply uttering these lines is usually not enough to break a spell of heartache, but the concept is on point, and so it has been amplified into powerful guided processes that allow one to fully experience and explore new reframed realities.

Chapter 9

Introduction to Techniques and Guided Processes

The techniques are written out in full with word-for-word instructions and with upfront commentary on their purpose and how they work. While most of the techniques are guided processes, such as guided meditations, some of them are exercises with step-by-step instructions. For the guided processes, I recommend using the audio recordings available to you, as described below. As an alternative, you can have someone you trust read them to you and serve as your guide.

How to Use the Audio

Audio versions of all of the guided processes are available for download in mp3 format at www.HeartBreakTherapy.com. Simply navigate to the downloads page and enter the password "healheartnow" to gain access. I highly recommend using the audio tracks for these processes. Using the audio tracks not only reduces the amount of work you have to do, but it is also likely to bring you a greater depth of experience. I recommend you fully read through each process before you choose to use the audio version. Knowing what the process involves can help you decide if it is appropriate for you, given your current set of beliefs, thoughts, and emotions.

How Do these Techniques Work?

To understand how these techniques work, we need to take a look at how our minds and emotions work.

As mentioned earlier, the psycho-scientific community has not yet reached a consensus on how the human mind works, but several models have been suggested. I don't want to bore you with theory, so I'll keep this brief by simply describing the model we are using for the techniques in this book. The first component involves the interrelationship between beliefs, thoughts, and emotions.

We are working under the following concept: Your beliefs about yourself and the world around you determine what thoughts you have about yourself and the world around you. Your thoughts then in turn determine the emotions you generate about yourself and the world around you. You then experience your emotions as feelings in your body. To simplify:

Beliefs → Thoughts → Emotions → Feelings

We will refer to this as B→T→E→F.

So as we look at heartache, which of these four components are we dealing with?

We are certainly dealing with all four. However, you may not be aware of all four. Most people are acutely aware of their feelings and emotions, some are aware of the thoughts underlying their emotions (although they may not realize that the thoughts are causing the emotions), and a very few are aware of the beliefs that underlie both their emotions and their thoughts. There are also people who are completely unaware of even their emotions.

Some will argue that emotions spontaneously generate in responses to situations and that there is no underlying thought. Those who make this assertion are only taking into consideration their conscious experience of themselves. Many of our thought processes are automated and are carried out by the subconscious, which operates below our conscious awareness. Those who argue that no thought comes first have not explored their own subconscious through hypnosis, meditation, or other insight practices.

Bringing the discussion back to B→T→E→F, emotional healing requires tracing emotions back to thoughts and then further back to the underlying beliefs.

This first phase of the healing process involves self-exploration and self-reflection, which lead to self-understanding. I think of this process of peeling back through the layers of feelings, down to thoughts, and further down to beliefs as "emotional archaeology." We are digging down within our histories to come to an understanding about what an existing psycho-emotional structure (such as a fear or an anger) was originally founded upon. As with archaeology, each layer we reveal gives us more clues about the nature of the underlying layer. The feeling gives us clues about the emotion. The emotion gives us clues about the thought. The thought gives us clues about the belief. As you move down through the layers, you are collecting self-knowledge. As the familiar phrase goes, "knowledge is power." Once you have acquired self-knowledge, you have the power to start making changes.

Within the B→T→E→F model, heartache is typically experienced as a mix of feelings, emotions, and thoughts. Heartache tends to hit very strongly on multiple levels and makes us feel completely overwhelmed. But let's break this down into more manageable pieces.

Every emotion has a corresponding feeling in the body. Typically we experience these feelings in the torso, with the most common manifestations being in the gut, solar plexus, chest, and heart. You may literally experience an aching in your heart area, which could result in a rapid or irregular heartbeat. You may have a tight chest, which could feel like a panic attack or heart attack. You may have a pit in your stomach, which could cause loss of appetite or nausea. The emotion is the on-the-surface outcropping of what is lying deeper within. Nearly everybody feels emotions in the body.

Perhaps you are also aware of your thoughts. People who have learned self-awareness through psychotherapy (being asked to reflect upon themselves) or who have practiced meditation are more likely to notice the mental chatter or self-talk that occurs in their minds. For those experiencing heartache, some typical thought patterns include:

- "I'm not good enough."
- "I'll never find someone."
- "I'll always be alone."
- "I'm not lovable."
- "I don't deserve love."
- "I'm too . . ." and insert your favorite self-insult here. Physical insults, such as fat, ugly, bald. Insults related to your mind, emotions, or personality, such as stupid, emotional, unstable, negative, judgmental, lazy, uneducated.

Beliefs are our deep inner interpretations of ourselves and the world around us. Sometimes beliefs are highly correlated to our thinking, such as "I'll always be alone" and "I don't deserve love," but other times they are too deep for us to easily consciously perceive.

A classic example is someone who experienced the divorce of their parents during childhood, and then internalized a belief that relationships can't last and that they only end in pain, bitterness, loneliness, and financial disaster. Someone with that belief system is likely to find reasons to sabotage his or her relationships, either right in the beginning or right when it is starting to show real promise of developing into a meaningful partnership. Someone with this pattern may have no idea why his or her relationships never work out.

The average person does not take responsibility for their experiences in life, as it is all too easy to lay the blame on others. Often, the individual never considers the possibility that they have a destructive inner belief about relationships that is causing all of their relationship failures.

Beliefs are held in our subconscious minds. We don't choose our beliefs in any given moment; rather, our beliefs are hardwired within us. However, with self-reflection through journaling and meditation, and with the tool sets of hypnotherapy and NLP, we can learn to rewire ourselves, we can come to understand our desires, and we can become conscious of the factors that go into our decision-making.

In order to effect real change in our emotional patterns, we need to shift our beliefs. How do we shift our beliefs? One way is through first identifying existing negative beliefs and then replacing them with positive beliefs. Identifying existing beliefs can be done through self-inquiry, although that requires learning how to do it and having the focus and energy to take ourselves through that process. This can also be done through a devoted meditation practice, wherein the more we calm our conscious mind and go within ourselves, the more the true nature of our subconscious reveals itself to us.

More easily, this identification of existing beliefs can be done in a therapeutic setting. Much of the work that hypnotherapists do involves identifying existing limiting beliefs, dissolving their often erroneous and irrational roots that usually date back to childhood, and then replacing them with expansive, positive, and supportive beliefs. It can be thought of as "psycho-surgery," that is, going in to find the cause of the emotional disruption, removing it, and putting in something new that is emotionally nourishing.

But instead of being in a therapy session, you have a book in your hand and access to audio files online. Fortunately, identifying the specific belief is not always necessary to create powerful change. Positive beliefs around the topic at hand can be created and then "imprinted" onto the mind.

This book is designed to create positive beliefs about yourself and imprint them onto your mind. Depending on how you view the reprogramming of beliefs, these techniques can be thought of as canceling out, replacing, or neutralizing the negative beliefs that have been holding you in a state of heartache.

Let's Get Started

Each process described in this book includes an introduction that provides an overview of the technique, the intended effect, and some ideas to take into consideration when deciding whether to use a particular process. Depending on your personality, philosophy, and current emotional state, some techniques will be better suited to you than others. I encourage you to read the introductions and then select the process that speaks to you most. Read through the entire process, and if you feel comfortable with it, download the appropriate audio file from the website and allow me to guide you through.

Make sure to be kind and patient with yourself as you embark on this journey of self-healing. Loving yourself fully and completely is the most important thing you can do for your healing process.

I'm sure you're feeling better already!

Chapter 10

Process 1: Selective Thought Mapping

Most of us experience our thoughts as a stream of consciousness—a never-ending chain of thoughts, one reminding us of the next, which reminds us of the next, and so on. Emotional turmoil and worrying is generally a negative set of thoughts that we return to over and over again, like a tape loop. We generally act as passive receivers of our thoughts, with our subconscious feeding us a continual data stream of interpretations, reactions, and warnings about the world around us and ourselves. When this data stream turns negative, we are flooded with negative feelings and then become the victims of our thoughts.

One definition of hypnosis is "a narrowed state of focus." A purposefully selected focus on thoughts of your choosing puts you in control of your reactions and interpretations. Actively choosing the content and quality of your thoughts is like taming the wild beast of the mind. It is like pruning the tree that has become unruly.

By pursuing an exercise of active, engaged focus on a healing perspective of your relationship, you are engaging in self-hypnosis. Concentration and focus, combined with a certain set of thoughts, has the effect of downloading those thoughts from the conscious mind into the subconscious.

Such focused and directed thoughts carry much more power than the original, scattered thoughts. And as the scattered thoughts bubble up through the pipes from the underground subconscious, by engaging in this form of self-hypnosis, you are essentially sending positive thoughts back down the pipes. Negative thoughts can be thought as sewage backing up from the sewer into the house, and actively engaging in positive thoughts is like pouring Drano down the pipes, clearing the thought pathways and the emotional body.

The Selective Thought Mapping technique is about choosing positive, supportive thoughts. While you're focused on a positive thought, you can't effectively think of a negative thought. Of course your mind can dart back to something negative for a split second here and there, but if you are fully engaged in an exercise that is asking you to create positive thoughts and write them down, you're likely to spend the majority of the time focused on positive thoughts.

Selective thought mapping involves a writing exercise where you start with a blank sheet of paper, and you write down only the thoughts you choose to have. Here's what thought mapping does for you:

- Gives you relief from the heartache-default negative self-talk
- Directs your attention to thoughts that you are choosing to have (shifting out of being a victim of your thoughts)
- Flexes the brain muscle that allows you to choose your thoughts—a very powerful skill that makes it easier for you to choose thoughts from now on
- Allows you to observe how your emotions shift when you choose to have positive thoughts
- Harnesses the concept of a blank canvas upon which you are painting the picture of your choice, anchoring in the knowledge that you have the power to create your mental and emotional reality in the present and the future

You can do multiple Selective Thought Maps. I have laid out a few of them here. You can do whichever ones feel comfortable for you, if not all of them.

Gratitude Thought Map

1. Take a blank piece of paper.
2. In the middle of it, write "I am thankful for . . ."
3. Fill the page with all things in your life that you are thankful for. Write down every aspect of your life that is working, especially those aspects that are thriving. Keep writing down

more and more, filling the page as much as you can.

4. When you feel satisfied that you have captured most things for which you are thankful, stare at the center of the page where it says "I am thankful for . . ."
5. Breathe deeply and allow yourself to imagine feeling very thankful. (Here's a secret: if you imagine feeling a certain way, you'll automatically actually feel that way.)
6. Allow your eyes to wander across the page, landing gently on each item that you wrote, triggering images of your happy, functioning life, and continually feeding your sense of gratitude.
7. Continue to breathe deeply and say to yourself, "I am thankful, I am thankful, I am thankful." You are literally reprogramming yourself and that is a beautiful thing.

"Not for Me" Thought Map

If you have been hung up on your ex even though you know that they were not right for you, then this process may work best. It is common in heartache for the mind to say, "I know he was bad for me," only to have the heart respond, "but I love him anyway!" Chemistry can be so strong between two people that it overpowers all logical decision-making. We can be hooked into a bad relationship like we can be addicted to a drug.

In fact, researchers using Functional Magnetic Resonance Imaging (fMRI) technology have shown that the brain activity of a person who is devastated from a breakup looks just like the brain activity of an addict who is in withdrawal from cocaine. Indeed, there is a very real biochemical and physiological aspect of falling in love that is known to researchers as "limerence."

Limerence is described as an involuntary state of mind that seems to result from a romantic attraction to another person combined with an overwhelming, obsessive need to have one's feelings reciprocated. Limerence can also be thought of as infatuation, which is associated with increases of norepinephrine and dopamine levels in the brain; it is the bliss and euphoria of a new romance. Limerence is a primal expression of attraction that manifests through physiology and brain chemistry. It causes the "love is blind" experience, resulting in people often putting a new potential lover on pedestals of perfection and semi-godlike status before they even get to know him or her.

While limerence has primarily been studied in terms of emotions and psychological experiences and behaviors, we know that emotional states are inextricably linked to brain chemistry. Thus, experiencing limerence is literally like taking a mind-altering drug that makes people crazy, take risks, and open up to great emotional vulnerability. Limerence tends to subside when love is requited, allowing the limerent party to either settle into a healthy relationship or to have a new clarity regarding their partner and suddenly see the character traits that make them incompatible as a long-term partner. When love is not requited, the limerent individual often becomes obsessive-compulsive and engages in desperate measures, such as stalking.

Some individuals are more likely to experience limerence than others. In my experience with hypnotherapy, I have noticed that people are more likely to experience limerence when they had childhoods where parental love was lacking. Each new potential relationship throws them back into the desperate and raw emotions of a child who is starving for love and willing to do whatever it takes to win the parents' attention. People who are otherwise emotionally strong and successful in their adult lives can spin out of control each time a new relationship presents itself. The real healing here that needs to be done with such people is to heal the pain from the lack of love during childhood. Hypnotherapy is one of the best ways to achieve this healing.

The primary researcher into limerence used interviews and questionnaires to understand the condition. It was found that the average limerent reaction duration, from the moment of initiation until a feeling of neutrality is reached, is approximately three years; however, the extremes were found to be as brief as a few weeks or as long as several decades. This is further validation that you should not at all feel ashamed of what you are experiencing—being emotionally out of control, having obsessive thoughts, being depressed—these are all part of a recognized and documented common human experience.

It is important that you be patient and compassionate with yourself. Your suffering is both imaginary and real, just like a dream at night is imaginary, and yet evokes very real feelings while you are experiencing it. Fortunately, you have the tools in your hand to alleviate this suffering.

In a way, when you are hung up on an ex who you know was bad for you, it is not your head fighting your heart as much as it is your head fighting your chemistry. And as we know from psychiatric medicines, chemistry and thoughts are intrinsically linked. Understanding that there is a physiological component to "love addiction" can help you to reduce the intensity of any perspectives you may have been holding along the lines of your ex being the love of life, your soul mate, etc. You can attribute at least part of the intensity of your attraction to that person to being the result of a very primal biochemical impulse that evolved in humans to help them stay together through pregnancy and to propagate the species. But just because the experience of love can be measured by scientists in chemical terms, it does mean that chemistry is the cause of all love attraction, and it does not mean that a pharmaceutical solution is the best way to address such states of emotional intensity.

Psychiatrists like to say that when we are anxious or depressed we have a "chemical imbalance." We often interpret this to mean that we have some kind of neurochemical defect that needs to be medicated. While in some rare cases this may be the case, the vast majority of the time we are simply experiencing emotions within the natural human spectrum, and since the realm of the psychiatrist is pharmaceuticals, their main lens through which they view emotions is through levels of neurotransmitters. If we are stuck in a state of anxiety or depression related to the breakup of a relationship, it is unlikely that we have an inherent chemical imbalance and it is much more likely that we simply have not yet come to peace with the change in our lives. Brain chemistry is the biochemical manifestation of emotions, and vice versa.

If someone is stuck for a long period of time in heartache-related anxiety or depression, then the beliefs and thoughts surrounding the breakup need to be examined and addressed.

Balancing and correcting unbalanced and ungrounded feelings is done by refocusing on reality, and specifically on a selected version of the reality that emphasizes the direction we want to move in. Following the Belief → Thought → Emotion → Feeling model, we use thoughts to generate feelings. While we aren't always aware of the subconscious thoughts, we are always aware of the feeling. And so generating feelings is accomplished by generating thoughts. Since two opposing feelings generally don't exist in the same moment, such as love and hate, we can eliminate an undesirable feeling by creating an opposing desirable feeling. Since we are more of a cerebral cultural than an emotive one, people generally find it easier to work with thought generation as a means of emotional generation.

This can be thought of as neutralizing a subconscious thought-feeling complex by actively engaging in the opposite thought-feeling complex. Like using thoughts and feelings of safety to neutralize thoughts and feelings of fear, we can use thoughts and feelings of dissonance and dislike toward the ex to neutralize a psycho-emotional obsession. There is often a truth that we know at the front of our minds (conscious level) that we don't know at the back of our minds (subconscious level). Hypnosis is often about downloading our consciously chosen desires from the front of our minds into the subconscious back of the mind so that those perspectives then become embedded, automatic, and permanent.

The "Not for Me" thought map is about getting down on paper, all in one place, all of the ways in which your ex did not resonate with you, so that the deeper part of you (the part of you that still clings to the relationship) finally gets the message that this relationship was not meant to be and that you are better off moving on.

In the center of this page, write the name of the person you have been experiencing heartache from, and follow it with ". . . is not for me." Fill the page with all the aspects of that person that make her or him "not right" for you. You are imprinting your mind with the idea that this person is not right for you and that, therefore, you are not losing out, there has been no loss, and you should be thankful this person is no longer in your life in the way they he or she once was. You can include anything that comes up—bad with money, sloppy, rude to waitresses, smelly, whatever!

If you end up feeling anger, disgust, or superiority, just let that be. These are all temporary states on your path to empowerment and healthy, balanced, and compassionate disconnection. Don't judge your judgments; let them serve you for now. Remember, you are practicing selective thinking to achieve a specific purpose—your happiness—which should be your number one goal (if it is not, then you will want to look at how you are not loving yourself fully and completely). You are doing no harm or injustice to your ex for going through this exercise.

"Better Off" Thought Map

This thought map focuses on the ways in which your life will expand or otherwise invite in new opportunity through being single once again. Start with "I'm better off now because . . ." in the center of the page and then fill the page with as many forward-looking opportunities as you can see for yourself. Think about things you may have sacrificed or compromised on during the relationship that you are now free to return to in your life. Think of other life choices that are opening up to you now that you are single again, such as changes in occupation, living location, lifestyle, daily patterns, health and wellness, hobbies, friendships, and even romantic relationships.

Fill the page with as many opportunities as you can,

and with each note, see a doorway of opportunity to your future. Look at each item with a spark of possibility in your eye, feeling like you're getting back on track with whom you really are and what you really want to be doing in your life. Keep returning your gaze to the center of the page, reaffirming how you are better off now.

Finish the map feeling a sense of relief that you are out of the relationship and that you are in a much better position to move forward into a bright and open future of your choosing and your creation.

"What Was Gained" Thought Map

What was gained from the relationship? What have you learned and how have you grown, even through the break up? Start with "I gained . . ." in the center of the page and then fill the page with as many things gained as you can think of. This includes things you have learned about relationships, love, the world, and yourself. It includes the good aspects of yourself that the relationship brought out, latent talents that were brought to the surface, needed skills that you developed, ways the relationship inspired you to be better, how you became a more well-rounded or whole person, or how you learned to live under some kind of extreme condition, which in turn added one more rich experience to your life's résumé. Include the things that the relationship exposed you to that you wouldn't have otherwise experienced alone, how it expanded your understanding of the world or some aspect of it. Where you traveled, what you ate, who you met . . . anything and everything you gained, grew from, or learned through the relationship.

Keep returning your gaze to the center of the page, feeling more and more satiated with each item you are consciously stuffing into your bag of soul goodies. Finish the map feeling like you're overflowing with rich experiences and a sense of thankfulness for the relationship having happened.

Chapter 11

Process 2: Reframing to What Was Gained

One of the most challenging aspects of heartache is feeling like the victim in the situation. This victim mentality takes away the power to heal. Feeling like a victim is common among those who experience extended periods of heartache and who have trouble finding the power to move on. Indeed, it is often the victim mentality itself that holds individuals back from being able to move on. Holding in one's mind the image and feeling of being a victim is, by its nature, disempowering, because the victim, by definition, is the loser in the situation. The victim was compromised, violated, dominated, tricked, deceived, lied to.

Feeling like the victim is wallowing in one's own weakness. We all fall down, but those who succeed are those who stand right back up and keep moving forward. Life is trial and error. We all make mistakes. It is through mistakes that we learn our greatest lessons. Acknowledgment of error is a key step in self-reflection, but it need not last longer than a moment before moving on to what was learned, gained, and how one will do better next time.

Alternatively, one may respond to heartache with anger, with a hunger to gain power, and with an obsession to "win" the battle. The anger response is common among those who are afraid of feeling their feelings. Vilifying one's ex-partner is a common escape mechanism from having to reflect upon one's own responsibility in the perceived failure of the relationship. This classic blaming of others is a childish response that gives a false sense of personal power. Maturing emotionally is largely about taking responsibility for one's own actions and the consequences of those actions.

Laying all the blame upon an ex-partner through insults and character judgments are false acts of self-exaltation. This self-aggrandizing is false because:

- It is based on the weaknesses and misfortunes of others and is not related to any inherent strengths of the one doing the self-inflating.
- It reflects a poor sense of judgment on the part of the proud and angry person. It is the one doing the judging who chose to not only enter into the relationship in the first place but also to stay in that relationship as things became toxic.

Holding this position is inherently hypocritical and is counterproductive to self-reflection and the personal growth that would otherwise naturally follow. Holding a judgmental and angry position may simply be a symptom of emotional immaturity, or it may represent a defense mechanism that results from a fear of feeling one's own feelings. It is critical to healing to be brutally honest with one's self when working to come to closure on a breakup.

> Since [narcissists] deep down feel themselves to be faultless, it is inevitable that when they are in conflict with the world they will invariably perceive the conflict as the world's fault. Since they must deny their own badness, they must perceive others as bad. They project their own evil onto the world. They never think of themselves as evil. On the other hand, they consequently see much evil in others.
>
> —*Scott M. Peck*

Holding an angry position to suppress or distract from feelings of heartache does not make the heartache go away. To deny the emotions of heartache by using anger requires selectively filtering reality, filtering out the sadness and filtering in the anger about the partner wronging you. To maintain this artificial stance of anger is to deny one's role in the relationship, and it blocks the critical step of at least partial responsibility for the outcome.

In some cases, anger does have an important role to play in the process of healing from heartache. Anger is a barometer of justice. We feel angry when our reality is not in alignment with our values of what is "right." If you've been feeling like a victim in your breakup, anger can be an appropriate emotional response to help you move into a position of personal power. People who have a difficult time feeling or expressing anger often find themselves perpetually disempowered, feeling like they have been the victim of injustice, but they are not willing to get angry enough to do anything about it. Anger moves us to action, to fight for justice. Justice for you—someone with heartache—means making yourself feel better. Justice for you means having your life back. You may need to get angry to find the power to act and bring justice into your own life.

People who have challenges feeling angry are also often split between feeling like the victim, on one hand, and making excuses for the perpetrator, on the other hand. This split can result in emotional paralysis, resulting in a spinning cycle of regret, guilt, and shame.

Many of the New Age spiritual perspectives tend to label certain emotions as "dark" or "negative," and this results in people feeling shame around their guilt, fear, and anger. In reality, all of these emotions are our teachers. We only need to learn how to extract the lessons from these emotions and then to release them.

People in the new thought movement, or subscribers to "staying positive," often won't allow themselves to get angry because they believe they should have compassion for their ex, even if the ex behaved in inappropriate and disrespectful ways. Having compassion for the person who wronged you is not going to help you while you are feeling weak and victimized. Compassion has its place later down the road when you are feeling strong and when you have a healthier perspective and stronger emotional foundation.

Feeling your anger can bring you out of victim mode and into a feeling of power. This is especially important if you feel that there was an injustice done to you. Make sure you are taking responsibility for all that you can in the breakup, but if you still feel truly wronged, then anger is an okay place to spend some time.

However, in the long run, neither anger nor the victim mentality is a useful place to stay if you are looking to complete a healing process. A solution to both of anger and victimhood is to focus on what was gained from the relationship and to move into a place of acceptance and thankfulness for what has transpired. You may be asking yourself, "He wants me to be thankful amidst feeling all this pain or anger?" It may sound like a far-away emotional state when you first imagine it, but I assure you, it is closer than you think.

If you are experiencing either victim mentality or anger, the first step into your power is through acknowledging that on some level, you yourself put yourself in that position due to the B → T → E → F relationship. Generally, we get ourselves into unhealthy situations due to emotional decision-making. If our emotions are the result of thoughts and beliefs based in unhealed pasts, then of course we are more likely to make unhealthy choices.

Acknowledging your past's role in your emotional makeup and in your decision-making is taking responsibility. When you take responsibility, you put yourself in a position of power. Having power is having the ability to choose, to select among a series of pathways and outcomes. You can choose to heal your past and thereby reconfigure your emotional decision-making framework.

Once you realize that you have choices, you have laid the foundation for making choices. Know that in this moment, you have choices—choices in perspectives. Know that you have been living from a perspective that has made you suffer, and now you have the ability to try on another perspective, a perspective that will free you.

Here's why this approach of reframing to what was gained is so powerful: if you think about the relationship that just ended and focus only on what you gained from it, then you will feel like you are coming out of the relationship as the winner. Each moment that you are focusing on what you gained is a moment you are not feeling anger or frustration toward the other person. Each moment that you spend feeling thankful is a moment you are feeling empowered and peaceful.

By following this process and holding a focus, you are introducing a new perspective into your belief system. The new perspective will automatically change your thoughts from what they have been, and your emotions will automatically be softer around the issue.

As you focus on all that you gained from your temporary companion in life, including your improvements in self-awareness and self-development (how the relationship pushed you into really examining yourself and increasing your self-awareness), you are finding a place of gratitude for that person. Your greatest growth in life takes place during the most difficult times, hence the term "character building" given to tough experiences. As you begin to view the most difficult aspects of the relationship as being the most productive for your own growth, then you can really let go of the negative emotions associated with those parts of the relationship. Of course this is an idealistic perspective to have, and many work their whole lives trying to develop this way of looking at relationships. Getting there by conscious effort requires incredible work and persistence, but through hypnosis, new perspectives can be adopted quickly and effortlessly.

Transcript of Process 2:

Make yourself comfortable and supported by lying down or sitting in a reclined position. Close your eyes. Breathe slowly and deeply.

Allow your awareness to go into your sense of hearing. Listen for all of the background sounds around you in your environment. Listen to each sound individually, one by one, knowing that they are just part of the background sounds and that as part of the normal background sounds of this environment, you can let them go; they can fade away outside of your awareness. One by one. Nothing can bother you. Nothing can disturb you.

Notice any sensations in your body. Notice how your weight is supported beneath you. Notice if anywhere is feeling uncomfortable and do anything you can to be more comfortable. Notice what areas feel warm or cool. As you acknowledge each sensation, know that these are the background sensations for this experience, and since they are background sensations, you can let them go; they can fade away outside of your awareness. One by one. Nothing can bother you. Nothing can disturb you.

Now imagine that your consciousness, your mind, your awareness, is floating up and out of your body, looking back upon yourself. In this free-floating state, you are completely free from the heaviness of the body, you are free from the emotions, and you are free from the thoughts. You have completely disengaged from your entire normal being, and you are now simply this beautiful, neutral, peaceful awareness. You look down at yourself, and you can sense the flurry of thoughts and emotions being felt down there. Down there, far away from you. You are safe; you are at peace, floating above, pure awareness.

From this peaceful state, you can examine anything in your life with complete objectivity, complete neutrality. From this perspective, turn your attention to the relationship from which you have recently been released.

See or feel a timeline in front of you with the past on the left and the future on the right. Along that timeline, see the relationship as an oval shape laying on its side—gradually beginning at one point on the left, taking up part of the timeline as it widens and expands in the middle, and then tapering off to a point of closure at the other end. See the relationship as a being or an energy unto itself. It is not you, yet it is something you moved through. Something you dove into and that you emerged from—like you were walking along a path, from a meadow, into a forest, which is the relationship, and eventually emerging back into a meadow.

As you remain there, floating and peaceful, neutral and objective, you see the relationship for all of its qualities. You are now going to focus upon what was gained from the relationship. Whether you experienced the relationship as good or bad, blissful or painful, it doesn't matter. What you are focusing on here is what you gained from it. This means what did you learn, and how did you grow? Or, as you are learning to put the relationship behind you now, what are you learning now, and how are you growing now? How did the relationship teach you to be wiser or stronger? What wonderful aspect of yourself was brought to the surface or developed through having this relationship?

And focusing on what you gained, how will you be a better person moving forward because of what you gained? How will you be stronger because of what you gained? How will you feel safer because of what you gained? How will you be kinder because of what you gained? How will you be more trusting because of what you gained? How will you be more joyful because of what you gained? How will you be more loving because of what you gained? How will you be a better person now?

See this person you were in the relationship with as being a tour guide for showing you around a specific area in your life. A guide you hired for a specific period of time to show you certain aspects of the world, or of yourself. There were specific things you needed to learn and specific challenges you needed to experience in order to grow and become a more whole person. See this person as coming into your life in the way that he or she was meant to, showing you the things that some deeper part of you wanted to see.

Now see you finishing the tour with new gifts of self-knowledge and a worldly perspective. Know that because of this tour, you are going to be better able to relate to others who have had similar experiences—that you will now be a better friend, a better family member, a better lover, and simply a more complete human being.

While this is the end of Process 2, you can easily stay just as relaxed as you are now if you wish to continue on to Process 3, Spiritual Reframing.

Chapter 12

Process 3: Spiritual Reframing

This process is an extension of Process 2. The introductory relaxation portion of Process 2 is not repeated at the beginning of the audio track for Process 3, so you can listen to these two back-to-back for full effect.

Spiritual Reframing will be comfortable for you if you are open to concepts of the soul, the afterlife, reincarnation, or "soul contracts."

Soul contracts describe the concept of our souls making agreements with other souls prior to beginning a lifetime. The agreements are generally about when we will enter one another's lives and what we will teach one another here on the physical plane of existence. It is similar to the concept of soul mates, but it is expanded with a greater perspective, since it involves agreements between many souls that come through one's lifetime. Some spiritual belief systems purport that the people who are the most challenging to us are our greatest teachers. Often these characters take the form of love partners.

This process is a guided visualization that provides a larger perspective (a soul perspective) on what you are experiencing and shows you that:

- Amidst the pain, there is always growth and learning.
- The relationship and separation were meant to happen.
- The partner you have broken up with is actually, on the soul level, someone very close to you who has agreed to interact with you in the way that he or she did so that you could learn something (and you, therefore, will be reunited and are indeed still together in a spiritual sense).
- On the soul level, you chose for this experience to happen for your own growth and development.

Transcript of Process 3:

Now imagine yourself as this floating, neutral awareness, hovering above your body. You are imagining yourself as your soul, your spirit. Allow yourself to float up higher and higher, and instead of looking down upon yourself in physical space, you are looking down upon yourself sitting on the timeline of your life.

See your past stretch out in one direction, with your birth at the end and your future in the other direction with your gentle passing back to spirit at the other end. As you, your own spirit, view this entire lifespan in one sweeping vista, you see that you are the orchestrator of this life. From where you are floating, all of time is at your fingertips. You can go into any point along the timeline and play in that reality. From where you are currently floating, linear time is an object that you can play with. Simply by desiring to be at a so-called "time" prior to your birth, you can be there. So be there now, prior to your birth, the hovering spirit that you are.

As part of preparing to be born into this life, you are making agreements with other souls. These other souls are friends and teachers of yours, whom you are inviting into your upcoming life to teach you things. And as a spirit, you know very well that humans learn best through challenge and through direct experience. You want a life that is rich with learning and powerful spurts of growth, so you are inviting some of your beloved soul friends to come into your life in all sorts of cloaks—as abrasive teachers, bullies, controlling bosses at jobs, obnoxious neighbors, manipulative friends, even unloving parents. You are inviting each of these characters into your life's plan so that you can learn all kinds of lessons in life, but mostly the lessons are to do with love.

All of these characters challenge you to either love them, despite how they are acting, or to love yourself, despite how they are treating you. The entire purpose of this life is to learn to love purely and deeply, how to love yourself fully and completely, and how to love others despite their own limited vision and emotional challenges. You are casting the characters in the movie that will be your life.

And see at this time the soul of this recent romantic partner of yours. This soul is a dear and beloved soul friend to you. You have interacted in many lifetimes together, and your bond will always be a beautiful one. This soul is highly skilled at playing difficult characters for you—characters that get under your skin and push your buttons. See yourself making an agreement with this soul to enter your life this time around as a romantic partner, and see yourself asking them to challenge you in the exact ways that you were challenged in this relationship.

Now to help you to know what to ask them, in terms of how to challenge you, reflect back for a moment on what it was you gained from the relationship. Now, knowing your spirit planned this before this lifetime, imagine being back in spirit, knowing that you need to learn this lesson. And now, imagine telling that soul friend that you need to learn this with their help, and tell them how you plan to benefit from them challenging you.

How is having them play this role for you going to teach you to love yourself more or love others more? See you shaking soul hands with this soul friend of yours, and then you going on your way, diving into that baby's body to be born with a veil of amnesia about this spirit world you are temporarily leaving behind.

Now, from that neutral floating space, see your life moving along that timeline, going into that relationship, becoming uncomfortable, stretching, expanding, feeling raw, vulnerable, parts of you breaking down and changing, and then leaving the relationship feeling very beaten down.

Then see yourself moving along the timeline, healing and becoming stronger than ever before in whatever way you have identified as being a gain for you from this relationship.

See your life being more open to love for yourself and others than ever before and feeling a great sense of thankfulness for the relationship having taught you that. See yourself at the end of your life's timeline passing back into spirit and reuniting with your soul friends who played roles in your life. See yourself shaking soul hands once again with that soul who played this recent romantic partner of yours. You are thanking them for a job well done, and you are promising to return the favor sometime.

As a spirit, you feel complete. You feel whole. You feel loved. You feel supported. And you feel connected to all that is.

This is the end of Process 3.

Chapter 13

Process 4: Releasing Emotional Enmeshment

This is a process that is best done by either listening to the recording or having someone you trust read the process to you. It is done standing up, with your eyes closed, in a space where you feel comfortable.

Transcript of Process 4:

Stand with your eyes closed in a quiet and comfortable space where you will not be disturbed. Take a deep breath. Relax in your position.

Imagine that you are a very powerful being that has the ability to create life by sculpting it out of clay.

Imagine that right in front of you is a large mass of clay waiting for you to sculpt it. With your eyes closed, use your hands to sculpt the body of your ex in the air in front of you. Imagine the extra clay falling away as you carve out the shapes of the body. Move from the head, neck, and shoulders down to the arms, torso, waist, and hips, down the legs, and finally to the feet.

Come back up, eyes remaining closed throughout this process, to face your creation. Take your hand in the air and hold the chin of your ex. Lovingly blow the breath of life into the mouth of your ex, imagining him or her coming to life.

With an awareness of sensations in your body, and feeling an emotional connection to this person, notice where you feel there are energetic cords of attachment connecting the two of you. You can move your hand down in front of yourself, from head down to hips, to sense where you feel connection. If you don't literally feel any cords, then just imagine where they might be.

Acknowledging that your energies are enmeshed together, you want to undo these connections so that you are both free. Imagine that each cord of connection is a little white string. Some of the strings are yours and are tied onto parts of your ex, and some of the strings are your ex's and are tied onto parts of you. First, untie all of the cords from your ex that are tied to you. As you untie them, see them falling and hanging loosely from the body of your ex.

Now untie, one by one, your cords that are attached to your ex. See and feel them hanging loosely from your body.

Imagine your ex moving backward away from you, becoming dimmer, smaller, and softer.

Turn a quarter turn to your left and sculpt out of clay your Future Self. This Future Self is highly spiritually evolved, very happy, confident, and is living life freely and fully. Breathe the breath of life into your Future Self.

Take the loose strings of love connection that are hanging from your body and connect them to the corresponding locations on the body of your Future Self.

Feel the energy flowing between the two of you. Feel your focus and energy fully invested in your Future Self. Notice that you and your Future Self are breathing in synch, sharing the same breath.

Look over your right shoulder and see your ex disappearing into the distance. Your ex looks over their shoulder back at you, smiling. They are also connected to their Future Self. You know that they are okay, and they know that you are okay. Turn back toward your Future Self.

Put your hands on the shoulders of your Future Self and pull them in toward you. Allow the two of you to merge into one whole and complete being.

Breathe deeply, feeling strongly connected to yourself, strongly invested in your future, and bring your awareness back to your surroundings.

Chapter 14

Process 5: Returning to Your Glory

This process takes you back in time to points where you were fully engaged, passionate, loving and feeling loved, trusting, open, adventurous, and joyful. It will remind you that you have been happy and fulfilled in your life prior to meeting your ex. In the visualization, you will experience being back in those states through an imagined situation, and this will bring those positive feelings into your present.

By experiencing these positive feelings here and now, your entire being will feel that you are capable of being whole and happy, now and always. This also teaches that you have a huge wealth of internal resources (positive feelings) from your past experiences and that they can be brought into the present to serve you here and now.

Transcript of Process 5:

Sit or lie in a comfortable position where your body can fully relax. Close your eyes. Take a few deep breaths, nice and slowly.

Think back to a time in your past when you were single and you were very happy. This may be many years ago . . . it could be back in high school or even earlier. Scan your life memories and find a point where you felt most engaged in life, most excited about something you were doing, most loved by those around you, most appreciated for who you were and what you were doing. Consider times when there was something that you were involved in or doing that you really enjoyed—a hobby, a job, an activity. Think of any natural talents you have and consider times when you were exploring or using those talents.

If you haven't settled on a specific time period yet, take a few moments now to settle on one. Don't worry about finding the absolutely perfect memory—any old good time will work just fine.

Now allow yourself to imagine being back in that memory. You are fully traveling back in time and getting into the body you had at that time, getting into the mind you were thinking from at that time, and getting into the heart you were feeling with at that time. As you become that person, you feel all that you were feeling at that time. Allow the feelings to come flowing into you. Allow the thoughts to come through your mind. You are being saturated with the enthusiasm, joy, love, excitement of that time and place. It is here within you now.

Now that you are feeling the way you were feeling then, imagine that there is a dial in front of you like a dimmer switch. That dial controls the intensity of these wonderful feelings and emotions. Imagine that the dial is now at 1 on a scale from 1 to 10. Imagine taking your hand out in front of you and turning that dial from 1 up to 10, feeling the power of the positive feelings and emotions ramping up within you. 1, 2, 3, 4, 5, 6, 7, 8, 9, 10. You are now at 10, and you are absolutely overflowing with amazing feelings and emotions. You are feeling more than you can contain, and you have so much amazing energy.

Bask in these feelings. Imagine that they are seeping into every cell into your body, into your DNA. Molecules are moving and shifting and realigning. Everything is being reprogrammed within you for joy, passion, enthusiasm, and happiness—for feeling that you have so much love in your life, that you have more than you need. These changes in your energy and in your body are permanent. You have an infinite source of energy and enthusiasm within you. You are your own source for love; you are self-sufficient.

I'm now going to count from 1 to 10, and as I count from 1 to 10, allow yourself to move forward in time with all of those amazing emotions within you. You are going to move forward in time to a place one month into your future from today. You will fully experience yourself in your life one month into your future from today, completely happy, energized, and enthusiastic. 1, 2, 3, 4, 5, 6, 7, 8, 9, 10. Good. Let it flow through you. Be your amazingly happy and fulfilled future self.

Now step back out of your life timeline so that you can see your entire life as though it were a piece of string laid out in front of you, with your past to the left and your future to the right. Now, with your imaginary hands, take the excited point in the past along the string, and take the amazing place one month into the future on your string, and tie them together. Cut off the loop of the "in-between" string that formed, and then run your magic fingers along the string so that the knot is smoothed away and the entire string is one continuous string of happiness and fulfillment. Feel a deep sense of relief at this continuity of happiness.

Think of an image to symbolize this deep sense of happiness and fulfillment. Imagine it fully—its color, texture, density, and temperature. This symbol is infused with all of your happiness and fulfillment. Any time you think of this symbol, it will remind you of all of these wonderful feelings, filling you with happiness and fulfillment. Simply thinking of this symbol brings you back into the wonderful state of being that you are in now. You can think of this symbol any time you need a boost, and it will respond with instantly shifting you back into these good feelings.

Now, as I count once again from 1 to 10, slowly and gently and lovingly bring yourself into a fully wide-awake and refreshed state, bringing all of this amazing peace and fulfillment with you. 1, 2, 3, 4, 5, 6, 7, 8, 9, 10.

Chapter 15

Process 6: Re-imprinting Your Ex

This process is an extension of the elephant/red balloon example discussed earlier. It takes a negative, emotionally charged image (your ex) and a positive, emotionally fun image and bonds them together so that your mind can no longer access the emotionally heavy image without also accessing the emotionally light image. The effect is that when you think of your ex after this process, the emotional charge associated will be reduced. There are a few ways of thinking about how this happens. I discuss a couple of them below.

One model is that our brain works like a filing cabinet. When you think of your ex, your brain goes to the file on your ex, and part of that file contains all of this heavy emotional stuff related to how badly things went in the end. By overlaying a fun, positive image, it is creating a new fun, happy file and merging that file with the file of the ex. The next time your brain goes to grab the ex-file, it is also grabbing fun and light images. Since you can't experience sorrow and playfulness at the same moment, the net effect is something between the two—something close to neutral.

Another way to look at this is from the perspective of neural pathways in the brain. Imagine that thinking about your ex creates a chain of neurons to be activated, creating a certain pathway that ends in triggering negative emotions. By thinking of a fun, light image, you are activating a completely different pathway that ends in triggering positive emotions. By overlapping the images, you are programming your mind to associate the images together, so that now when you think of your ex, both pathways are being activated, and both negative and positive emotions are triggered. The mix of negative and positive neutralize each other, essentially allowing you to think of the ex without an emotional charge.

Transcript of Process 6:

Close your eyes. Take a deep breath. Continue to take deep breaths, imagining tension and stress and heaviness leaving your body through your exhales. Good. Breathe.

Now think of an image that is really funny to you. Something silly and playful. It could be a penguin doing a wobbly walk; it could be Bart Simpson, SpongeBob SquarePants, Barney, anything silly at all. And now think of some silly music, such as circus music, "Old MacDonald Had a Farm," or any song that as you listen to it makes you feel light and happy. Now that you have an image and a song, bring the two together. Make the scene moving and active and alive. If you have chosen a character as your silly thing, make them dance around to the music. Add any other elements that make it sillier to you, that make you want to chuckle at how ridiculous the whole things looks.

And now insert your ex into the scene. See your ex surrounded by all this silliness. Lots of dancing, singing, music, colors flying around. See your ex holding hands and dancing with any silly character in your scene, light and silly and having fun.

Now, with the music continuing, see your ex's face up close, and see all the funny characters dancing on your ex's cheeks, across your ex's forehead, down your ex's nose, over your ex's lips, and across your ex's chin. The funny characters are all having fun and stomping all across your ex's face and your ex has this big smile, having a good time amidst all the silliness. Allow yourself to find the whole scene quite ridiculous and feel laughter welling up inside you too.

From now on, whenever you think of your ex, you also see these characters dancing all over his or her face, and you'll also hear the silly music playing, drowning out any thoughts you are having. From now on, when you see your ex, you have a feeling of fun and ease and lightness.

Chapter 16

Process 7: Blowing Bubbles

This process can be used for any thought that is consuming more of your mental time and energy than you would like. It could be used for thinking about your ex, your job, your finances, your health, or any aspect of your life that is not feeling harmonious.

Our minds typically obsess over that which is not working in our lives at any given point in time. It is easy to lose perspective; we forget about all that is working and allow the challenging aspect of our lives to become all we focus upon, thereby overwhelming us. As I discussed earlier, the mind can only think about one thought at a time, and so the more we think about what is not working, the less we can see what is working. Obsessing over a small aspect of one's life that is in disharmony expands the feeling of disharmony across one's entire being.

This process is about acknowledging that there are many different aspects to your life at any given point in time and bringing all aspects into awareness so that the one part that isn't working well at that moment feels smaller and more manageable. The process helps to externalize the disharmony, reframing the part that is not working so that it is merely an aspect of your present experience, not an actual part of you.

The process creates a perspective where you observe a great deal of space around you, and each aspect of your life is a little bubble floating within that space. A job bubble, a relationship bubble, a health bubble, a financial bubble, a family bubble.

Firstly, making the disharmonious bubble the same size as all of the other bubbles makes it feel smaller and more manageable. Secondly, by seeing multiple bubbles at the same time floating in front of you, your focus is diversified across the bubbles, thus bringing you a healthier and balanced perspective. And thirdly, by seeing the bubbles out in front of you, it communicates to your subconscious and your emotional self that the disharmonious aspect is something you are observing outside of yourself and that it is not you that is in disharmony.

Transcript of Process 7:

Sit or lie in a comfortable position where your body can fully relax. Close your eyes. Take a few deep breaths, nice and slowly.

Now imagine that you have a bottle of soap for blowing bubbles. And you have a little plastic wand to blow them through. Choose a color for the bottle. Choose a color for the wand.

Now, think of your physical health, in general, and any issues that come up around that. Now bring the soapy wand up toward your lips and blow a bubble filled with all of your health issues. The bubble is only three inches across, and it hangs out in midair about three feet in front of you. The bubble is very strong and stays intact throughout this process. All your health issues and thoughts about your health are now contained in that bubble and are no longer inside of you.

Now, think about your finances. Blow a new bubble, filling that bubble up with all of your finances. Allow the bubble to be around the same size as the first bubble and to settle into position near that first bubble, but with plenty of space between them.

Now, think about your family. Blow a bubble with all of your family members and have that bubble find its own place in front of you.

Blow a bubble for your ex. Allow your ex and everything associated with that situation to have its own bubble. The bubble is small, tight, and strong, and it finds a suitable location amidst the other bubbles.

Blow bubbles for anything else that your mind spends a lot of time on. Your job, your boss, a friendship, a hobby, a commitment . . . keep blowing bubbles until you feel you have been emptied of all thoughts and concerns.

Now see that there are many bubbles in front of you. And the bubble with your ex in it is simply one of many, equally sized bubbles. See all the bubbles out in front of you at once. You have the ability to focus on any one of them. As you focus on one of them, they move toward you and come into clear, detailed focus. And then, at your command, you are able to pull your vantage point back out to see them all at once.

You are the master of your life. All of these components make a rich and diverse life experience for you. You have complete choice over where to spend your time, how close to allow each bubble to get, and how much energy you want to put into each of them. Know this deeply: you are in control. You are the master of these bubbles. You can expand them, shrink them, or make them go away. If any of them still feel uncomfortable, imagine that you can touch them with your finger and shrink them down to whatever size you choose.

Chapter 17

Process 8: The Spinning Technique

This technique is about shifting your emotions through shifting the feelings in your body associated with those emotions. We will be using imagery and metaphor to communicate to your subconscious to make these shifts. There is some overlap with Process 6 (Re-imprinting), but this process is working from a different angle. In the B → T → E → F relationship, we will be working only with feelings. Since we are working at the superficial level of feelings, this technique is not likely to shift the underlying beliefs, and thus the old thought patterns are likely to return in the future.

The Spinning Technique is not a core *HeartBreak Therapy* process, but it is a versatile technique that can be used for any feeling in any situation. Since there are multiple emotions that can combine to form the undifferentiated soup of heartache, the Spinning Technique can be used to tackle individual emotional triggers and imbalances. For example, if you are feeling lonely, the first step in this technique is to scan your body and notice how loneliness feels in your body. Identifying that physical feeling is the key to releasing that sensation and thereby dissolving the emotion.

Transcript of Process 8:

Identify the physical sensation associated with the negative emotion you are experiencing. Note the location. Pit in the stomach? Tight chest? Nausea? On a scale from 1 to 10, with 10 being most severe, note what number you think the intensity of the feeling is. Remember that number.

Give that feeling a spinning motion. Imagine that the feeling is a spinning disk of energy in your body.

Now imagine moving that disk of energy out in front of your body, about 2 feet in front of you.

Notice what color the disk seems to be. Now change its color to something more pleasing.

Notice which direction the disk is spinning in. Now reverse the direction of spin.

Now clear your mind and think of a time when you were having a lot of fun and felt really happy. Amplify those good feelings; feel them stronger and stronger.

Now take those feelings and pour them into the disk that is the new color and new spin direction.

Make the disk spin faster and faster; give it more energy. Decorate it and give it more color and vibrancy. Feel the positive feelings coming off of it.

Now bring the disk back into the area of your body

that it came from. Feel that whole area absorb all of those good feelings.

Now you are complete and you can open your eyes. Try to think of the initial negative feeling. Try to feel it in your body and see what the intensity of it is on the 1-to-10 scale. This is how you measure your progress. If you would like to further reduce the feeling, go through the process again.

Chapter 18

Process 9: Developing Self-appreciation

Non-supportive relationships and difficult breakups can cause us to lose our sense of self. We can forget about all the positive traits we have and easily focus on the negatives. This process scans your life for positive traits, good deeds, accomplishments that make you proud, and positive feedback you have received throughout your life. Any of these positive memories are considered to be inner resources that you can draw upon to bring you strength, peace, and confidence in the moment.

Transcript of Process 9:

Sit or lie in a comfortable position where your body can fully relax. Close your eyes. Take a few deep breaths, nice and slowly.

Think now of all the aspects of your personality that you really like. What makes you unique? What do people value in you? What are you particularly good at? What comes easy for you? Identify these aspects one by one, making a mental list. It could be your sense of humor, your reliability, your consistency, your listening skills, your punctuality . . . anything along these lines that fits for you. Make this list very familiar to you.

Repeat these traits over and over so you have a solid grasp of all of them and so that you can keep them all in your awareness. Allow yourself to move from seeing and knowing these traits intellectually to feeling a great sense of appreciation, thanks, and gratitude for having these wonderful aspects as a part of your being.

Now think of all the good things you have done for others over your lifetime, starting from when you were a kid. How were you giving? How were you generous? How were you kind? Moving forward into your teen years, how were you giving? How were you generous? How were you kind? And as an adult? How have you been giving? How have you been generous? How have you been kind?

Allow all of these memories of selflessness and generosity to expand in your awareness now. Allow them to overwhelm your perception. All you can see is how wonderful you have been to others. Feel a deep sense of contentment with the good person that you are. Know that, to the best of your ability, you have lived your life with dignity, respect, and honor.

Now think about things you have been proud of throughout your life, accomplishments that have given you great satisfaction. First scan the memories through your childhood. What great achievements did you have there? What bright spots were in that period? And now your teen years. What accomplishments were there? What are you proud of? And in your adult years. What did you overcome? What did you make it through? What did you achieve that you are proud of?

Now bring all of those accomplishments into your field of awareness all at once. You are filled with a sense of accomplishment and pride and fulfillment. Know that you have made it through many challenges in your life and that you can be proud of the life you have led.

Finally, think about all the wonderful things people have told you about yourself throughout your life. Think back to your childhood. What positive words did your teachers say about you? What about your parents—did they have supportive or positive words for you? What about other relatives? Grandparents? Aunts? Uncles? What positive remarks did the adults make about you when you were a child? Now, move forward to your teen years. What did your friends appreciate about you the most? What did your teachers have to say about you that was positive or supportive? What compliments did people pay you? What did people envy about you? And now in your adult years. What do people appreciate about you the most? What compliments do you receive? What do people envy about you? What makes you unique and special in the eyes of others? What are some of the most profound compliments or expressions of gratitude you have received from friends? What about coworkers and bosses? How have they appreciated you? What about your family? Now that you're an adult, how have they shown their appreciation for you?

Allow yourself to experience all this lifetime of appreciation in this very moment. Feel yourself surrounded by a circle of all those whose lives you have touched during your life. See them surrounding you in a circle of love and support. This is a ceremony to honor YOU, and they are all, at once, expressing their gratitude and telling their stories of what you did for them that was so wonderful. You are fully open at this time, and you are receiving all of this love and appreciation.

Now, all at once, you can feel all of the aspects of yourself that you are thankful for, and you feel that gratitude. And you know all the ways in which you've been kind and generous in your life, and you feel that, to the best of your ability, you've lived your life in dignity, respect, and honor. Also, you know that you have made it through many challenges in your life, and you are feeling proud of the life you have led.

On top of all that, you are surrounded by the love and appreciation of everyone whose lives you've ever touched. All the nice things anyone has ever said about you, you are hearing now. You are open, and you are allowing all of this positive love and support to pour down into the core of your being. It is filling you up and reminding you that you are a vibrant and whole person just as you are. You are surrounded by love and support, and your life continues to be a wonderful and positive adventure.

When love is lost, do not bow your head in sadness; instead, keep your head up high and gaze into heaven, for that is where your broken heart has been sent to heal.

—Author Unknown

Chapter 19

Process 10: Developing Self-love

This technique is about eliminating negative feelings you have toward yourself and moving into loving yourself. A relationship breakup can result in many negative feelings about yourself, through either believing negative things your partner may have said about you or through blaming yourself for the failed relationship. This process helps you to move toward fully loving yourself through transforming your feelings about individual aspects of yourself and moving them from a place of being rejected into a place of being embraced. This allows you to move toward emotional wholeness and complete self-love.

The technique offered here should be repeated until all known self-rejected aspects of you have been treated. The process can be repeated for individual aspects, as well. Becoming more aware of your emotions will help you to assess where you have remaining judgment and rejection.

Before you begin this technique, ask yourself which

parts of yourself you are not in agreement with, or, in other words, which aspects you would like to be different. I recommend that you make a list of things that you don't like about yourself and keep track of these aspects as you move through and repeat this exercise. Keep coming back to the items on your list until you are able to think about each aspect of yourself with a sense of peace.

Transcript of Process 10:

Sit or lie in a comfortable position where your body can fully relax. Close your eyes. Take a few deep breaths, nice and slowly.

Imagine that you are holding in your arms some creature that you feel a great deal of love for. It could be a baby or perhaps a small animal. Notice the unconditional love you feel for the being you are holding. Notice that even though the being may be flawed, or weak in some way, you still love it completely and without question. Notice how your heart feels as you focus on that feeling of love. Notice the feeling of love expanding in your heart and how that flow of love feels in your body.

Now think about somebody you don't like. Imagine holding a baby-sized version of that person. See that person with his or her insecurities, weaknesses, and what you may consider to be his or her "flaws." From a loving and compassionate perspective, imagine that you are a wise, old being, capable of seeing the good in anyone and seeing the pain in anyone. Imagine now that flow of love coming from your heart and flowing to him or her. Imagine holding a small version of that person in your arms and sending them the same unconditional love that you sent the original object of your love.

Now bring your attention to an aspect of yourself that you do not like. This could be a character trait, such as pride or vanity, or a specific situation that keeps occurring in your life, or even a memory from the past. You can choose anything that brings you feelings of unease or dissatisfaction, or perhaps something stronger. With your open, loving, and flowing heart, imagine that you are holding that aspect of yourself in your arms. Send love to that aspect of yourself. Feel and perhaps see love flowing from your heart to this aspect of yourself. You are saturating that aspect of yourself with love and bringing it to rest . . . bringing it into peace and acceptance.

Open your heart more and more. Know that that aspect of yourself is actually part of who you are, and as such, by loving it, you are loving yourself. You want to love yourself, and the only way to fully love yourself is to love this aspect of yourself. So it is easy and natural for you to let that love flow.

Chapter 20

Moving On to New Love

What better benefit is there in getting over heartache than to be open to love once again? Loving doesn't always have to end in heartache. We don't have to lose our identity in our loves. We don't have to pour all of our love into one person.

To love healthfully and sustainably, we need to love intelligently. Love intelligence is related to the larger concept of emotional intelligence, which is all about adaptability, flexibility, the ability to try on different perspectives at will, and to reframe life's situations to healthier interpretations as needed. Loving intelligently is about starting with a baseline of strong self-love and diversifying both the sources of external love and the targets of your love.

Chapter 21

The Three Kinds of Love

The heart is a transceiver of love, both transmitting and receiving love. As such, to love fully, love needs to flow into you and out of you. A fully diversified love life includes an active flow of three kinds of love: inflow, outflow, and self-flow.

Inflow

Inflow is the kind of love we receive. It flows into our hearts from the world. Inflow is the first kind of love that we come to know after birth. We typically first experience an inflow of love from our mothers after our birth. Inflow is then generally expanded to other family members, including our father, grandparents, aunts, uncles, and siblings. If we have a strong foundation of inflow love from our families, then we tend to be more confident and comfortable out in the world. A strong and diversified inflow makes us feel secure and supported.

When parents are consumed with their own mental or emotional issues, when they are consumed by addiction, when they are engaged in abuse, or when they are simply too busy to spend enough time with their children, the lack of inflow into the child is akin to a malnourishment of love. The child feels forgotten, abandoned, ignored, and deprioritized.

As children we tend to personalize the events in our lives; that is, we blame ourselves for the misfortunes that befall us. A child who does not receive abundant support and love from his parents often concludes that he is undeserving of love, unimportant, worthless. As innocent and misguided as this interpretation is, if it is not corrected, it often remains with the individual through adulthood, resulting in a lifetime of low self-esteem. This lack of foundational inflow love, combined with the resultant low self-esteem, often leads to patterns in adulthood of relationship codependency and sabotage.

Codependency is a desperate grasping for a love that was never achieved in childhood. A codependent believes that since love did not come naturally as a child, it must be actively sought after to be received. He will also tend to believe that love is neither dependable nor consistent, since he has had no experience with such a kind of love. The codependent behavior is an attempt to manipulate a person into giving them love and to control the love so that it does not slip away. This desperation, combined with the low self-esteem, usually results in a need for inflow that is so great that the codependent often does not discern the quality of the relationship.

Just as the worst food can taste good when we are

famished, a dysfunctional relationship can be deeply addictive to a codependent once some semblance of an inflow has been established. This desperation is usually obvious to those observing the relationship from the outside, and unless the codependent's partner is of a similar emotional makeup, this behavior often drives the partner away. When the codependent is abandoned by their partner, their beliefs about being undeserving of love or incapable of having a relationship are further enforced.

Sabotaging behaviors are also rooted in a deep sense of being unworthy of the love one is receiving. When one feels unworthy, one is naturally led to believe that the affection they are receiving from their partner will not last. The saboteur lives every day in fear of an impending breakup and the perceived inevitability of once again being unloved and feeling alone. From a subconscious desire to feel in control of the situation and to end the relationship before the partner can do it, the saboteur destroys the relationship.

In some cases, the saboteur knows what she is doing in the midst of her action, while other times her behaviors are subconsciously driven and she acts out of her normal character. Saboteurs often look back at their actions that led to the dismantling of a relationship and are bewildered as to why they lied, cheated, or became unreliable, since it worked contrary to their conscious desire to make the relationship work. Whether saboteurs are sabotaging consciously or unconsciously, rarely can they help themselves from carrying out the impulses that are driven from within and that are designed by the subconscious to avoid reliving the pain of childhood.

Damage from lack of childhood inflow is primarily formed with respect to parents, but it can also be contributed to when other family relationships break down, when friendships fade away, when those who love us die, and when romantic relationships come to an end.

Inflow is the kind of love most adults seek most. Some adults single-mindedly seek and demand an idealized inflow experience to the exclusion of outflow and selfflow, and it is understandable how this happens.

Firstly, inflow is the foundational love of the mother that is necessary for healthy psycho-emotional development and long-term stability, and yet so many us do not get that foundation. With the increases over the past few decades in the divorce rate, in the number of single moms, and in the need for women to generate an income, mothers are under greater stress with less time to bond with their children than ever before.

These challenges on motherhood have often compromised the quality of care that mothers in Western society can provide to their children. Due to these conditions, an increasing proportion of today's population has not had healthy foundational inflow established, and thus they move into the adult world with the desperate seeking described earlier.

Secondly, Western society has promoted individualism to such a degree that many have taken on the egotistical and spiritually disconnected notion of entitlement. "I deserve true love!" they exclaim. Many Western nations have not experienced war, economic depression, famine, or widespread natural disasters for several generations, resulting in a shift in cultural values away from humility, frugality, appreciation, and the interdependence of tightly woven families and communities and toward a sense of individual entitlement and unlimited potential for growth and success.

The idolization of material wealth through generations of corporate marketing to the masses has bred within us a future-obsessed and self-obsessed mindset, creating a culture of individuals hell-bent on achieving their "dreams," often without any consideration of how those plans might interface with the needs of their family, their community, the environment, or humanity at large. Even New Age thought movements, such as the Law of Attraction, have created forms of spiritual materialism, offering up a spiritual framework and justification for people to get what they want, when they want, and how they want it.

Many people today live with a vision of exactly what they want their life to look like, which largely distracts them from a present-centered awareness and appreciation of what they already have. This self-centeredness and sense of entitlement do not encourage, or even leave much room for, how a person can give to the others, contribute to the world, and engage in an outflow of love.

The combination of not having had our basic emotional needs met as children, combined with our societal programming of demanding what is "rightfully" ours, often creates an obsession with finding a "perfect" relationship—one that will satisfy our inner emotional voids and that will match the white picket fence image that our culture has fed us. This obsession with an idealistic imaginary future life serves as a constant reminder of how that imagined love is lacking in one's life.

The increased trend toward individualism and technological replacement of human interactions also exacerbates the lack of human connection and diminishes the baseline sense of inflow and outflow that happens when people engage in reality with one another and with their community. The amplification of the sense of disconnection from baseline love flow further feeds the fear that one's love needs will never be achieved.

The fear of being alone for the rest of one's life, or at least in old age, is one of the greatest outcroppings from this breakdown of interdependency in Western cultures, and this fear is often one of the main motivators in the modern desire for romantic love. While this fear is present to some degree even among most emotionally healthy people, it is amplified within those with a shaky foundation.

All of these conditions combine to create a modern culture that fuels an unhealthy and unsustainable inflow-focused approach to love.

Outflow

Outflow is the love we give. It flows out from our hearts into the world. As children, we experience outflow of love to our parents, our siblings, extended family, and our pets. As we grow older, outflow is usually expanded to include friends for whom we care deeply, as well as romantic partners. Outflow is our capacity to give and share love in the world.

Children learn healthy outflow when two criteria are met: first, they must have a baseline of healthy inflow; and second, they must have people or animals around them whom they consider to be loveable. There needs to be something worthy of loving in order for a heart to love it.

A completely loving yet dysfunctional parent could satisfy a child's inflow needs, but at the same time, the child could view this parent with great disappointment and even disgust. Such a child would lack the practice of returning love and could grow into an adult who sees him or herself as an emotional island, largely disinterested in love because they have never experienced the bliss that comes with its expression. Such a child may have fully developed self-esteem and be strong out in the world, but he or she may be unable to express or even feel love toward others.

Changing one's focus from receiving love to giving love almost always results in an epiphany about the nature of the heart and happiness. How many people have been transformed through bringing a child into the world and experiencing the incredible outpouring of love from themselves? How many divorcées have found a deeper and broader sense of personal satisfaction in life by throwing themselves into community work and sending their love out into the world for the greater good? How many people throughout history have had emotional and spiritual breakthroughs through a devotional practice of dedicating their love to a cherished deity?

To outflow love is to generate love. To generate love is

to fill one's self with love. When you are filled with love, there is no need for any other love, for you are already filled. To love is to be in ecstasy.

Spiritual devotees who experience a direct connection to their god(s) are referred to as "ecstatics." Ecstatics allow themselves to be filled with love. The love with which they fill is not a love received from their object of focus; rather, they are filled with the love that they themselves generate and allow to flow through them.

Such states of ecstasy can be reached with outflowing love for just about anything—a person, an animal, a tree or plant, a flower, a sunset, a rainbow, a force of nature, a piece of music or other sound, a god, saint, or angel, or any other of a multitude of things. This love can be cultivated by focusing upon anything in which one finds beauty or resonance through the senses or through the mind.

What's beautiful about the outflow of love is that once it is outflowing for anything, it tends to continue to flow for everything. This is like when someone falls in love and everyone around them says they are glowing. When a person is in love, she is more generous, more patient, more kind, and more loving. The outflow of love is not only for her lover, but for everyone and everything.

Self-flow

Self-flow, or self-love, is the kind of love we give to ourselves. It flows out from our hearts directly back into our hearts. As children, we learn self-love when our parents and other elders show us that we are lovable. We learn from our authority figures. If our parents and other elders treat us with love, then we inherently feel lovable, and we tend to grow up with self-love.

Self-love is how we feed ourselves. Self-love can sustain us when we are not actively receiving the love of others and when we are not in the active act of loving others. Self-love allows us to enjoy alone time, which is critical to developing self-awareness and self-knowledge.

Those lacking a healthy level of self-love have a hard time being alone; to them, alone time feels disconnected, isolating, and lonely. For such people, alone time is a torture they do all within their power to avoid. People who are uncomfortable being alone are often love addicts, seeking constant validation from their world and immersing themselves in distracting activities when they cannot find such validation.

> Our daily practice consists in running away. If we have a moment free, we will make use of it to watch television or read a magazine article so we will not have to go back to our [inner emotional] territory. We are afraid of the suffering that is inside of us, afraid of war and conflicts.
>
> —*Thich Nhat Hanh*

Self-love, which allows for alone time and contemplation, is a necessary baseline for personal growth and comprehensive spiritual development.

Following the B → T → E → F relationship, as we

develop a deep belief in our own value and beauty, we generate thoughts of self-appreciation, which give us the emotions and feelings of self-appreciation and self-love. If our elders didn't teach us to respect, appreciate, and love ourselves, then it is certainly a mandatory path to be actively and consciously chosen and walked if one wishes to become a healthy person who can have healthy relationships. Once self-love is established, a great amount of inner peace is developed, since the most fundamental of emotional and spiritual needs are then being met.

> The cyclone derives its powers from a calm center.
> So does a person.
>
> —*Norman Vincent Peale*

Self-love involves both inflow and outflow. As such, it is often the most difficult of loves for one to cultivate. A full expression of self-love requires a mastery of inflow and outflow, although limited expressions of self-love can still be experienced, especially among those who limit their external love interactions due to not feeling safe.

The ecstatic bliss described above in the discussion on outflow can also be experienced through self-love. This is especially true when one moves into the more mystical levels of love, when the boundaries between love-of-other and love-of-self begin to dissolve and the interconnectedness and oneness of "all" begins to be experienced.

The more you love, the more you know love. The

more often you love, the better you get at loving. The more loving you are, the more joy fills your life. The more you radiate love, the more love is attracted to you. When you gain mastery of love, and make love your primary spiritual practice, love will work for you and never against you. The more we all embrace love, the closer we will be to heaven on Earth. Until then, you can at least find the love within yourself, which will lead you to the personal heaven that awaits you within.

In closing, I would like to provide you with a final guided process (Process 11) that visualizes the healthy flow of the three kinds of love.

Transcript of Process 11: Flowing the Three Kinds of Love

Sit or lie in a comfortable position where your body can fully relax. Close your eyes. Take a few deep breaths, nice and slowly.

Feel yourself surrounded by a circle of all those whose lives you have touched during your life. See them surrounding you in a circle of love and support. They are all facing inward, facing you. The hearts of each of these people are glowing and vibrating with love for you.

As they are focusing their attention and their love upon you, the love in their hearts for you is growing and growing. Their hearts fill with so much love for you until their hearts can no longer contain the energy, the beauty, the joy. Their hearts begin to overflow, and the love comes pouring out toward you. The tendrils of love are coming toward you, toward your heart. The love wraps around you. The love envelops you.

All of these individual streams of love are collecting around you, holding you, embracing you, cradling you. The love is working its way into your being, finding its way through your back to your heart. Your heart has a back door that allows love to come in. All of this love collecting around you is flowing into your heart through your back. Feeding your heart. Nourishing your heart. Softening your heart. Healing your heart. Your heart is filling with love. Your heart is infused with love. Your heart is full of love. Your heart is overflowing with love. You are now in full receipt of the love that is already available to you in your life. You are receiving all of the love from your past and from your present.

As you receive all of this love, you feel and know that you must be lovable. You must be deserving of love. Your heart is now overflowing with love, and the love needs somewhere to go. Allow some love to flow out from your heart through the front of your heart, through your chest. Your heart has a front door that allows you to send love out. As the love flows out from your chest, it catches some of the incoming tendrils of love from those standing around you and rides the current around to your back and back into your own heart. You now have a flow of love out of the front of your heart, wrapping around you, and flowing right back into your heart through your back. You now have an established flow of self-love that continues to feed you, keeping your heart flowing and open and healthy and alive.

Now that your heart is filled, and now that your flow

is self-sustaining from your own self-love, any love coming into you is now excess love that you can share with the world. As love continues to flow into your heart, your heart continues to overflow.

All of that overflowing love needs a place to go. Allow that love now to flow out into the world. You can start by sending love to the people in the circle around you. As you send them love, see them receiving it and becoming happier and healthier and lighter. As your heart sends love out through your front, you find that it feels incredibly good to send love to others. Your heart grows bigger with all of this love flowing through it, and with this increased size of your heart comes an increased capacity to love.

Your heart is now seeking other destinations for your love. Begin to send love beyond the scope of those gathered around you. Send your love to people who may not be sending you love, but who you think could use some love in their lives. Send it to people you know or know of who are in pain and suffering and whom you would like to help. Send your love to them. Send your love to the spirits of people you know who have died. Send your love to a group or nation of people who have suffered from a natural disaster. Send your love to a group or nation of people who are currently in, or were recently in, a war.

Send your love to animals you know or have known. Send your love to plants and trees that you know or have known. Send your love to the entire planet, seeing the tendrils of your love wrapping the entire planet.

Your love is promoting peace, healing, and health

for people all around the globe. Your love is helping to preserve and protect animal life all around the planet. Your love is helping to protect and enrich forests on every continent. Your love is helping to purify the water in all of the lakes, seas, and oceans.

Feel that your love is being received, absorbed, and integrated into the planet. And feel the planet radiate a diffuse, all-encompassing, continuous vibration of love back to you, which anchors you, makes you feel in your bones that you are wanted and needed and that you belong right where you are.

Your heart is now in a full and healthy state of flow: receiving love from others and from the planet, sending love to yourself, and sending your love out to others and to the planet.

Your heart is a beautiful and perfect transceiver of love. In through the back and out through the front, love flows through this beautiful heart of yours.

Chapter 22

Psychotherapy and Psychiatry in Treating Heartache

There is a dearth of methods for the treatment of heartache. Heartache doesn't get media attention, research funding, or much scientific inquiry. It is commonly accepted that allowing one's self to be open to love is a risk that people choose, but it's one that can have unfortunate consequences.

Our society is fatalistic in its acceptance of heartache as a natural consequence of love. The devastating effects are continuously emphasized to us through various art forms, particularly music. The vast majority of the songs we hear on the radio are either about falling in love or having a broken heart. There is a mass commiseration that goes on related to heartache, with very little in the way of guidance for how to move on.

The mainstream approach to treating heartache is through psychotherapy with a psychotherapist and often also involves a psychiatrist prescribing medication to treat any related depression, anxiety, and insomnia. Prescribing medication can be powerful in terms of quickly shifting biochemistry and emotional states, hopefully avoiding suicidal tendencies and improving quality of life. However, it is at best a Band-Aid solution that buys time for the patient to process the life event with a more manageable intensity of emotions and hopefully move toward peace, and at worst it provides a numbing distraction from the real emotions that need to be moved through and which will only return full-force once medication is discontinued.

Considering the well-known wide array of side effects, the often long-term withdrawal symptoms of getting off of these drugs, and the rarer and often more serious effects of cross-drug interactions, psychiatric drugs are something that should be approached with tremendous caution. The decision to take psychiatric medication for depression should not be taken lightly, and the risks may outweigh the benefits in all but the most severe cases of depression. In many cases, the drug being prescribed is either not effective or only minimally effective for the symptom at hand, and psychiatrists are subject to individual bias and human error just as much as anyone else.

Human clinical trials of pharmaceutical drugs always include documenting patient improvement for those taking the drug in question, compared with a group of patients who take a placebo (sugar pill) disguised as the actual drug. The scientific establishment fully recognizes that the power of belief is very strong in patients, and that many have improvement in their conditions simply by taking part in a therapeutic process, including the taking of "medication," even if that medication is only in their imagination. The placebo effect is a wonderful and highly documented example of the healing power of the mind and literally demonstrates the power of hypnosis.

Many of the pharmaceutical products commonly prescribed today have been documented to have only a minimal benefit when compared with placebo. In a 2010 article in the *Journal of the American Medical Association*, researchers concluded: "Although the benefit of medications versus placebo is significant in patients with very severe depression, it may be minimal or nonexistent in patients with mild or moderate symptoms. Prescribers, policymakers, and patients could all benefit from being made aware of these important findings." (Fournier J. C., DeRubeis R. J., Hollon S. D., et al. "Antidepressant Drug Effects and Depression Severity: A Patient-Level Meta-analysis," *Journal of the American Medical Association* 303 (2010):47–53).

When a psychologist refers a patient to a psychiatrist, who can then prescribe medication, they are basically saying that the psychotherapy they are offering is not effective enough to address the true emotional needs at hand, at least not within the timeframe desired. The only remaining option is to prescribe pharmaceuticals that will quickly adjust the brain chemistry so that the emotions are not felt with the same intensity and the patient experiences some relief.

This is the challenge with mainstream psychotherapy—it is a greatly helpful tool at increasing self-awareness and undergoing gradual healing over periods of months to years, which can be fine for those seeking gradual growth and healing in their lives overall. However, the training that psychotherapists receive does not include active, solution-focused tools to bring about the rapid emotional healing and transformation that is often needed by people in emotionally distressed states, such as heartache. And so psychotherapists are working within a minimally effective framework, which is the perfect setup for them falling back on chemical solutions.

Medication may lessen the intensity of some of the symptoms of heartache, but it does not address any underlying psychology that may have played a role in creating a broken relationship in the first place, such as partnering up to avoid being alone, partnering to seek approval, being a poor judge of character, or being attracted to unhealthy qualities in someone. These are psychological and emotional dynamics that can be identified through psychoanalysis with either a psychologist or a hypnotherapist. Once identified, these patterns can be gradually chipped away over time through psychotherapy, or resolved quickly through the direct and targeted techniques of hypnotherapy.

Taking responsibility for our actions and feeling the full consequences of our choices are critical aspects to personal growth. Pain motivates change. Since medication can take much of the pain away, it removes much of the motivation for self-reflection, learning, and personal growth that comes with a natural course of heartache.

Medication can numb people through the most critical period of grieving and, while emotional processing and recalibration of the heart can occur while medicated, the personal growth and transformative aspect of that recovery will be muted. Once the worst of the grieving period is over and the medication is stopped, individuals who underwent this treatment are likely to return to the same old approach to life that set them up for an emotional disaster the time before.

Additionally, without having fully processed through the emotional experiences, the trauma of the heartache can remain in the body-mind system and manifest as anxiety, depression, relationship insecurities, as well as other mental and physical ailments.

Chapter 23

Further Reading and Self-development Paths

As human beings, we easily get stuck in a particular perspective that can limit our ideas, emotions, experiences, and our potential. Some spiritual traditions have the ultimate aim of teaching how to detach from individual perspectives, thereby freeing our minds from being stuck and liberating us into a state of clarity and awareness. Another, perhaps more approachable, remedy to getting stuck is to continue to invite in a variety of perspectives.

This section is intended to offer you a smorgasbord of books, audio courses, and personal development programs that offer a variety of perspectives and promote personal insight, healing, and power. I have provided my own brief descriptions here. If you want further information, take a look online and see what other readers, users, and practitioners are saying about these items.

Books

- ***The Wisdom of Your Subconscious Mind*** by John K. Williams. This book was written in 1973. It is out of print, but you can find used copies online. This clear, concise book inspires the reader by showing the depth and breadth of what is possible by learning to work with the subconscious. Williams conveys his teachings through compelling stories of famous historical figures and more obscure characters alike who harnessed the wisdom and power of the subconscious to achieve great things and have surprising, almost magical, phenomena result. The book provides a great overview that can serve as an excellent foundation for anyone wishing to explore their own potential.
- ***The Power of Your Subconscious Mind*** by Joseph Murphy. Originally written in 1963, this book is a self-help classic. A great companion book to self-hypnosis, this book highlights the incredible potential to transform nearly any aspect of one's life through working with the subconscious.
- ***Emotional Intelligence*** by Daniel Goleman. We've all heard the stories of the high school dropout who becomes a hugely successful entrepreneur. These tales are invigorating, speaking to an understanding that lives within each

of us that it is not the mind that is the greatest determinant of success in the world, but the heart. The author presents research on the brain and on human behavior to underscore how emotional intelligence is a stronger determinant of success in life than the traditional IQ. Goleman defines emotional intelligence in terms of self-awareness, altruism, personal motivation, empathy, and the ability to love and be loved by friends, partners, and family members. If these are areas of your life and your character that you are seeking to grow, this book is probably going to be a great read.

- ***Love, Freedom, Aloneness: The Koan of Relationships*** by Osho. Osho abandons traditional, and often limiting, notions of what it means to be in a relationship and provides a refreshing and in-depth look at how to maintain the self within a life shared with another. The book addresses healthy forms of love, learning to be alone without being lonely, and achieving personal emotional freedom both within and without a romantic relationship. The book is repetitive at times, and some of Osho's concepts of ideal relationships seem unrealistic, but still, there is much wisdom to be gained.
- ***The Myth of Freedom and the Way of Meditation*** by Chögyam Trungpa. Trungpa was a Tibetan Buddhist who fled Tibet during the

1959 Tibetan uprising against the Chinese communists. He came to the West, learned the ways of Westerners, and went on to become the most prolific Buddhist teacher in the United States. Trungpa's writing is clear and to the point. This book provides a wonderful introduction to the psycho-emotional challenges of the Westerner and then introduces Buddhist thought and a description of meditation practice with an explanation of how it can help to live our lives with more ease, joy, peace, and love.

- ***The Untethered Soul: The Journey Beyond Yourself*** by Michael Singer. Singer teaches the reader how meditation can be used to cultivate self-awareness, emotional freedom, and inner peace. The author dissects the nature of the self and lays out a clear rationale as to why we are not our thoughts, our emotions, or our beliefs, and teaches how we can live a life untethered from these restrictions.

- ***Many Lives, Many Masters*** by Dr. Brian Weiss. Dr. Weiss was a psychotherapist who was administering hypnotherapy with a small-town housewife who had never left the United States or had education beyond high school. When she started speaking in ancient languages and relaying historically accurate details from other lifetimes, Dr. Weiss was forced to expand his concept of reality. It's a short and fascinating read that offers an alternative view of human beings and what life here is all about.

- ***Destiny of Souls*** by Dr. Michael Newton. If you liked *Many Lives, Many Masters*, then *Destiny of Souls* is an excellent next read. Dr. Newton is a hypnotherapist, who had plenty of experience doing past-life regressions and was curious about what happened between lifetimes. His groundbreaking work is astounding and largely aligns with concepts that we also see in the traditions of Spiritism and Hinduism. *Destiny of Souls* is a wonderful book at helping to dissolve the reader's fear of death. Dr. Newton's commitment to detail and consistency is sure to make even the most doubtful reader ask some serious questions.

Audio

- **Philosopher's Notes.** Philosopher's notes is CliffsNotes for books on personal growth and spirituality. If you're a slow reader or just plain busy, then Philosopher's Notes allows you to get the golden nuggets of some of the wisest texts ever written in a twenty-minute audio clip or a six-page PDF. With well over one hundred notes already produced, Philosopher's Notes is a goldmine of wisdom and perhaps the best way to get quickly exposed to a wide variety of perspectives. Philosopher's Notes are like antioxidants for the mind: when our world feeds us a constant stream of free radicals through negative news, this is a great way to insert some positive thoughts and to learn skillful frameworks for dealing with both your own life and the world at large.

- **HoloSync**. HoloSync harnesses the power of brain science to allow you to achieve the benefits meditation with little effort in a short period of time. It has already been several decades when we learned that within seconds human brainwaves fall into alignment with the wavelengths of the music we are listening to. The technicians at Centerpointe Research Institute have made use of this "brain entrainment" technology to tailor a beautiful audio program that allows for the slow rewiring of the mind and emotions over a period of years. Old traumas are released, anxiety is dissipated, and peace is achieved. A more affordable and less formal option is a product called EquiSync.

Techniques

- **Self-hypnosis**. Self-hypnosis is a deeply healing method to cultivate inner peace, self-esteem, and self-love. It provides much of the same results as meditation, but in an easier, faster, and more direct manner. Learning self-hypnosis can open doorways to incredible amounts of personal power to manage your thoughts and emotions and, if you are open to it, to levels of consciousness in which you can experience all sorts of fascinating phenomena. You can learn self-hypnosis through books, online audio and video programs, or through a hypnotherapist either in person or via the telephone or web conferencing technology, such as Skype.

- **The Work** by Byron Katie. The Work is a technique of emotional liberation that is described in a book by the same name. The author teaches you four simple questions that you can apply to any emotional issue, guiding you to greater insight, self-awareness, emotional intelligence, and peace.
- **Sedona Method** by Hale Dwoskin. The Sedona Method is a technique to dissolve negative emotions and achieve peace and happiness that is described in a book by the same name. The Sedona Method says that all of us have peace and happiness at our core. We are covered by negative emotions and feelings. As we dissolve these negative emotions and feelings, we experience more and more of this peace and happiness.

- **The Silva Method** by José Silva. The Silva Method is the name given to a self-help program developed by José Silva. The method involves using "alpha" frequency sound beats to entrain the brain onto the alpha state, which is essentially light hypnosis. The Silva Method teaches users how to achieve this state and then how to use this state for self-exploration, changing thought patterns and stuck emotions, eliciting inner wisdom, and sending prayer/intention out into the world around us. The Silva Method basically teaches people self-hypnosis, but it also folds in aspects of mediumship (communication with spirits) and magic (focusing thoughts to affect reality).
- **The Journey** by Brandon Bays. This is the story of a woman with a large tumor on her ovaries who dissolved it by exploring the unresolved emotions stored in her body from a past traumatic event. While the focus in this book is largely to open up the readers' eyes to the mind-body relationship, the technique provided allows the user to find freedom from any stuck emotional state.

About the Author

Andrew Gentile has been helping to heal broken hearts since his work as a hypnotherapist began in 2003. From his personal experiences of heartbreak, he knows how the pain of losing a loved one can shut down the ability to enjoy life and to engage in the world. Through working with clients using hypnotherapy, Andrew has witnessed time and time again how quickly and easily most people can return to inner joy and emotional freedom when given the right tools. These experiences, in addition to his own recovery from heartbreak using these methods, inspired Andrew to share this powerful healing with the world.

Andrew grew up in Ontario, Canada, and lives between Toronto and San Francisco, California. He splits his time between his hypnotherapy practice and working as an environmental consultant for renewable energy projects across the United States. Andrew feels that both of these roles contribute to the healing of the planet and enjoys the balance of working in both the perceptual and physical realities. Enhanced through studies in permaculture design, Andrew enjoys working with plants and the earth and continues to notice the many overlaps and parallels between emotional and ecological health and healing.

In addition to his certifications as Hypnotherapist and Medical Hypnotherapist, Andrew also has a Bachelor of Science Degree in Biochemistry and a Master of Science Degree in Environmental Management. He has studied nutritional counseling, homeopathy, meditation, energy work, mediumship, shamanic healing, permaculture, and continues to learn from both his clients and his teachers.

Andrew can be contacted via the book's website, www.HeartBreakTherapy.com.

About the Illustrator

Robert Gentile is a Canadian cartoonist and illustrator. Robert's natural artistic talent and ability to translate human behavior and societal issues into thought-provoking cartoons were recognized early on. As a teenager, he was hired as editorial cartoonist for a weekly Canadian newspaper. After years of producing comical, and often controversial, cartoons on political, societal, and community themes, Robert temporarily put down his pen and ran for political office himself. After politics, Robert put his marketing and economics degrees to use first in the corporate world and later as a marketing consultant and business owner.

Robert maintains his political involvement through volunteer roles, advising, and helping out with various campaigns. Over the years, Robert has continued to channel his creative talents through private client cartoons, customized greeting cards, illustrations, and product concept designs. He is able to provide a versatile range of artwork styles to suit the needs of his clients. More information on Robert and his services can be found at www.RobertoIllustrations.com.

CPSIA information can be obtained at www.ICGtesting.com
Printed in the USA
LVOW10s0513071113

360225LV00006B/8/P

9 781626 523883